T0326359

Cambridge Elements ≡

Elements of Writing in the Ancient World
edited by
Andréas Stauder
École Pratique des Hautes Études-PSL (EPHE)

CYPRO-MINOAN AND ITS WRITERS

At Home and Overseas

Cassandra M. Donnelly
University of Cyprus

CAMBRIDGE
UNIVERSITY PRESS

Shaftesbury Road, Cambridge CB2 8EA, United Kingdom

One Liberty Plaza, 20th Floor, New York, NY 10006, USA

477 Williamstown Road, Port Melbourne, VIC 3207, Australia

314–321, 3rd Floor, Plot 3, Splendor Forum, Jasola District Centre,
New Delhi – 110025, India

103 Penang Road, #05–06/07, Visioncrest Commercial, Singapore 238467

Cambridge University Press is part of Cambridge University Press & Assessment,
a department of the University of Cambridge.

We share the University's mission to contribute to society through the pursuit of
education, learning and research at the highest international levels of excellence.

www.cambridge.org
Information on this title: www.cambridge.org/9781009517294

DOI: 10.1017/9781009381840

First published 2024

A catalogue record for this publication is available from the British Library.

ISBN 978-1-009-51729-4 Hardback
ISBN 978-1-009-38180-2 Paperback
ISSN 2753-6378 (online)
ISSN 2753-636X (print)

Cypro-Minoan and Its Writers

At Home and Overseas

Elements of Writing in the Ancient World

DOI: 10.1017/9781009381840
First published online: December 2024

Cassandra M. Donnelly
University of Cyprus

Author for correspondence: Cassandra M. Donnelly,
Donnelly.Cassandra@ucy.ac.cy

Abstract: Poised as middlemen between the Ancient Near East and the Aegean, writers of Cypro-Minoan, the undeciphered Late Bronze Age script of Cyprus, borrowed and transformed writing practices from their neighbors and invented new ones. Bits and pieces of the script are found throughout the Mediterranean, but there are few clay tablets, characteristic of neighboring scribal-based, administrative writing traditions. Instead, Cypro-Minoan writers wrote on mercantile objects, outside of scribal schools. As the administrative centers of the eastern Mediterranean collapsed c. 1177 BCE, administrative writing systems went with them. Cypro-Minoan remained in use, presaging the spread of the Phoenician alphabet. This Element explores the role of writing and trade during the collapse period and introduces readers to the Cypro-Minoan script, its history, and approaches to its decipherment, showing that writers of an undeciphered script can still communicate when we make the effort to look.

Keywords: Cypro-Minoan, Bronze Age collapse, trade, history of writing and decipherment, Cyprus

ISBNs: 9781009517294 (HB), 9781009381802 (PB), 9781009381840 (OC)
ISSNs: 2753-6378 (online), 2753-636X (print)

Contents

1 Introduction to the Cypro-Minoan Script

The Cypro-Minoan script is an undeciphered Late Bronze Age (1650–1050 BCE) script from Cyprus, a relatively unimposing but beautiful island located in the northeast corner of the Mediterranean. It is perhaps surprising that a script we cannot yet even read, from an island with limited name recognition outside of Europe, can help us understand the spread of the alphabet you are reading right now, but it's true. The Roman alphabet is ultimately derived from the Proto-Canaanite or Phoenician alphabet, as it is better known, which is one of the few Mediterranean scripts that survived the "Bronze Age collapse" (c. 1200 BCE; sometimes the date "1177" is used as a shorthand, Cline, 2021). The term "collapse" dramatizes a complicated process during which the administrative palatial centers, integrated into an international diplomatic and economic network, fell apart to be replaced by small-scale networks of overseas trade. Many of the scripts used in the administrative centers disappeared. Scripts apparently used by overseas traders, such as the Phoenician alphabet or the Cypro-Minoan script, often survived, but the use of these scripts during the collapse period is poorly documented in all cases except for Cypro-Minoan. A study of Cypro-Minoan reveals how people and traders on and off the island retained a dynamic script tradition that is interesting both on its own terms and as a proxy for imagining how the Phoenician alphabet survived and thrived in the post-collapse Mediterranean. Only through Cypro-Minoan can we reconstruct how traders used and disseminated writing, including the early form of our own alphabet, during the volatile collapse period.

Cyprus has always been a place of geopolitical significance. Throughout recorded history, the island has sporadically served as a battleground between larger powers, especially ones to its east and west, and sometimes was ruled by them. Today, it is the easternmost country in the European Union and the only European Union country that is technically located in the Middle East, perched atop the meeting point of the Eurasian and Anatolian Plates, just below the Turkïye–Syria border. It is also the only divided country and capital in Europe. The northern third of the country has been occupied by Turkïye since 1974. Though divided, Cyprus is also and always has been a linchpin, a place where European, Anatolian, and Middle Eastern cultures and interests mix and converge.

The significant role Cyprus played in the history of writing during the Late Bronze Age is often overlooked. Its writing practices are unusual compared to its neighbors and therefore hard to understand. The best-known scripts of the Late Bronze Age Mediterranean are the syllabic cuneiform writing tradition of Mesopotamia, famous for its clay tablets, and Egyptian hieroglyphs and hieratic, written on iconic stone monuments and papyrus scrolls. In third place, at a considerable distance depending on which country you were educated in, are the Aegean scripts of Linear A and Linear B, both notable for their clay tablets.

Writers of Cypro-Minoan did not care much for clay tablets. Nor did they write on stone monuments. If they wrote on papyrus, none survives. Instead, writers of Cypro-Minoan wrote on an assortment of objects, chief among them clay and metal vessels, clay balls, and bronze tools. Many were objects not originally created to serve as writing surfaces and would have been visible in daily life. Despite the apparent visibility of Cypro-Minoan writing, the number of Cypro-Minoan inscriptions, strictly defined as script signs used to record a word, is unexpectedly small, only around 300. But, as I hope to show in this Element, writers of Cypro-Minoan did not adhere to a strict definition of writing. Instead, they wrote on lots of different objects in different social settings, often writing texts with only single signs.

Exactly what they were doing with the single-sign texts is one of the themes of this Element. Are they simple abbreviations of words, meant to convey information, or are they similar to brands like the "B" on a Boston Red Sox baseball cap, ubiquitous in New England where I am from, meant to be recognized but not necessarily read? Or perhaps they are more like a graffiti tag, advertising the person or association responsible for the text's creation to an audience in the know. Whatever the case, should we consider the single signs writing, even if they do not record words and may not even be abbreviations? To a certain extent, the definition of writing depends on what we are trying to learn through its study.

1.1 What We Can Learn from the Study of Script

For the purposes of this Element, writing is comprised of two elements: script and language. Script is the material manifestation of a written communication mode, and language is the verbal manifestation of a spoken communication mode. Script and language can often overlap, but they are not the same (Vlachek, 1973). Think of how script can convey a change of meaning that is not spoken: It is conveyed through language but communicated solely through the manipulation of the material properties of writing, that is, the script. *When I italicize words*, for instance, I signal to the reader to pay *very close attention to the words I've just written* without using a change in language to do so.

The present Element is about *script*, not language. After all, Cypro-Minoan is undeciphered, which means we do not know the language or languages that the Cypro-Minoan script records; for that matter, we do not even know the language or languages spoken on Late Bronze Age Cyprus. Script is a material thing that takes on shape and form when people write it. In that sense, script is like any object of archaeological study. The inscribed object's material features – its archaeological context, its script, the materials used to write it, and what it is written on – become clues through which we can understand the social lives of the people who wrote the text.

There are certain things we cannot learn from the study of a script. For instance, a script is not an indicator of the ethnicity of its writers. Ethnic identity is a dynamic concept, which changes according to different social settings and historical time periods (Jones, 1997). Today, many people define their ethnic identity based on the languages they speak or the script that they write, but there is no inherent trait that links script to ethnicity. The problem of associating ethnic identity with script choice becomes immediately apparent when we think about the many different languages a single script can record, including ones geographically, historically, or culturally removed from the script's source. The Roman alphabet, itself derived from the Phoenician alphabet, is an example of a script that records a surfeit of languages unrelated by language family, region, or chronology.

The text you are reading uses the Roman alphabetic script to record the language American English. This same script can also be used to record, with small modifications, the languages of Polish (*Polski*), Basque (*Euskara*), Vietnamese (*Tiếng Việt*), Latin (*lingua Latīna*), and more. The speakers of these different languages or their political representatives chose the Roman alphabet as the script to represent their languages for a variety of sociohistorical and political reasons not often or always tied to ethnicity. The study of script is therefore most fruitful when it is a study of social and political history, which is the approach taken in this Element: The Cypro-Minoan script and the material features of the inscribed object and its text are a gateway for learning about its writers.

1.1.1 Document Forms

To focus our attention on the script and its writers, I have adopted the concept of "document form" as an analytical framework from the study of archival documents, a discipline called "diplomatics." A document form is defined as any text whose external physical features, such as the materials it is made of and written with, its formatting, and so on, conform to "rules of representation" (see Table 1; Duranti, 1989, p. 15). Rules of representation come into existence by virtue of being taught and reproduced in specific institutional settings, either formal or informal ones, from one generation to

Table 1 List of external material features of document forms

(1) Writing medium	Includes object type, material, size, shape
(2) Text placement	Where text is positioned on surface
(3) Text orientation	Writing direction (sinistroverse, dextroverse, boustrophedon) and writing position (e.g., vertical, horizontal)
(4) Writing instrument	Includes instrument material, shape of implement and tip, size, etc., but also whether inscription is made on hard or soft surface
(5) Punctuation	Includes word dividers, intra- and extratextual punctuation, abbreviations, etc.
(6) Sign sequences	Do the same sign sequences recur? If so, on one document form or several?
(7) Paleography and ductus	Includes sign shapes (paleography) but also shape and size of individual elements that comprise the signs
(8) Archaeological findspot	Are similar texts found in similar findspots, such as mercantile, ritual, funerary, administrative, etc.?

the next. A study of document forms is therefore also a study of the institutional settings in which writers produced texts. Unlike most archival documents, which were written on objects designed to be written upon, Cypro-Minoan often appears on objects produced for other purposes. In such instances, instruction and text production probably occurred outside of institutions like scribal schools, whose primary purpose was instruction in the production of texts.

A document form is not the same as writing medium. Writing medium refers to the type and material of the object on which writing appears. The clay tablet is one example of a writing medium. It encompasses a wide range of document forms, some quite dissimilar from each other. Compare the cuneiform culture clay tablet and Linear B clay tablet pictured in Figure 1. The cuneiform tablet has a "pillow" shape, compact rule lines, and tightly packed wedge-shaped sign components produced with a triangular or square-tipped stylus. The Linear B tablet is flat and rectangular with clear, wide rule lines

Figure 1 Comparison between Linear B and cuneiform tablets. Linear B Tablet PY Vn 10, cuneiform tablet from Anatolia, probably Kanesh, Met. 66.245.10.

Photograph of PY Vn 10 courtesy of the Pylos Digital Tablet Project, Palace of Nestor Excavations, the Department of Classics, University of Cincinnati.

and "linear" sign forms drawn with a bladed stylus. Both are examples of the clay tablet writing medium but different document forms. Their material features, from their shapes, line ruling, and writing implements to their formatting, are distinctive.

Institutional contexts play a defining role in dictating the rules of representation of a document form. In the cuneiform cultural world, instruction in the production of clay tablets was transmitted primarily in scribal schools. Surviving school texts indicate that scribal schools maintained similar curricula over a 3,000-year lifespan, spreading eventually from Mesopotamia to Anatolia. Scribes received training in how to construct clay tablets, which writing implement to use, and how to use it, with the result that cuneiform clay tablets show remarkable uniformity in construction, script, and formatting. Only experts can readily distinguish regional and chronological differences among tablets made in different times and places. How signs are drawn remains extremely stable throughout time (Taylor, 2015). Cypro-Minoan document forms, in contrast, are more varied, but their variations seem to occur within a rather narrow range. In other words, its writers followed rules of representation when constructing document forms, even on objects not purpose-made for writing. Take, for instance, the example of the vessel text document form (see Figure 2). Writers selected a rather narrow range of vessels to write on, often preferring to incise texts onto handles post firing (Hirschfeld, 2008). Formatting is restricted to horizontal or vertical placement along the handle axis, and most texts begin at the top of the handle before it bends. Variation is expressed in sign shape and the width, depth, and shape of incision lines. The adherence to a broad set of rules seems to indicate that writers of

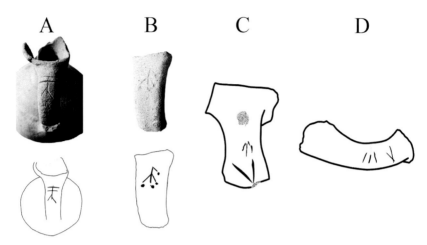

Figure 2 Examples of the vessel text document form. A. CM 20.199/ T1907_193; B. CM 1962_99; C. ##115 ENKO Avas 008, D. Melos inscription. Photographs and drawings by author, courtesy of the Cyprus Museum and the Department of Antiquities, Cyprus.

Cypro-Minoan received instruction in how to write and how to make document forms but not the strict training characteristic of scribal school education. One aim of this Element is to describe the nonschool institutional settings where writers of Cypro-Minoan practiced writing and to think about how writing can be transmitted outside of the school setting.

1.1.2 How We Define Writing Shapes What We See

The study of script can change the way we think about writing. Writing is often conceived of as a tool whose value derives from its ability to convey language in written form. Writers of Cypro-Minoan had a more nuanced practice of writing. Take the vessel text document form, once again. It includes around 100 texts labeled "inscriptions" by scholars of Cypro-Minoan because they contain multiple script signs in a row and therefore likely record a word in a language. In addition to the 100 inscriptions, there are over 1,500 single-sign texts. The single-sign texts comprise a mix of script and nonscript signs. Some texts with script signs probably record abbreviations of words, like the "B" on a Boston Red Sox cap mentioned above, but others were probably more similar to McDonald's golden arches, sharing the shape of a script sign but able to convey meaning regardless of whether its viewer could read its script. The nonscript signs, for their part, were perhaps more akin to the Nike swoosh, capable of evoking a clear association in their viewer without the use of writing. The writers of the vessel document form apparently did not erect strict barriers between script signs that record language and other signs. They used script signs to communicate something besides language and nonscript signs in a manner similar to script signs.

But what can writing be used for if not to convey language? Several East Asian countries have long-standing calligraphic traditions that appreciate writing for its aesthetic qualities, like any other branch of the arts. Brands and graffiti employ a mix of script and nonscript elements to convey extralinguistic information. While Cypro-Minoan texts have a certain beauty, it is not apparent that their writers cultivated an art of calligraphic writing. Branding and graffiti may be a better fit for explaining Cypro-Minoan's mix of script and script signs, but how do these very contemporary concepts translate into the world of the Late Bronze Age?

1.2 The Late Bronze Age (c. 1650–1050 BCE): Cyprus in Context

1.2.1 The 17–15th Centuries

The first Cypro-Minoan text appears long before the Bronze Age collapse, in the Late Cypriot I (LCI) period beginning roughly in 1650 if not earlier (see Figure 3). The 17th century on Cyprus marks renewed contact with eastern and western neighbors after a prolonged period of insularity. Increased extraction of agricultural and copper resources translated into increased social stratification and the concentration of population-dense towns, especially on the island's coasts. Enkomi, which plays a central role in the use of writing on the island, may have been the main power center on the island, controlling copper extraction in the interior of the island from the coast, or one among several regional powers. Trade with the Levant and Egypt was brisk, while mercantile connections with Crete and Cilicia may have been limited to the trade of precious oils or perfume (Webb, 2022).

The decision to begin to write may have been in response to renewed contact with neighbors, to internal social changes, or for no particular reason at all. There are no hard-and-fast rules for determining the circumstances under which people decide to invent or adopt a script. "Script transfer" is the process wherein a script is deployed to write a different language in a new context. Script transfer can come at the hands of an inspired individual/group or result from a cumulative process called "script diffusion" where adjustments and additions to a script happen slowly over decades or centuries (Salomon, 2021, pp. 153, 167). Often, script transfer results from a combination of a singular, conscious act of creativity followed by a long period of diffusion and reforms. The

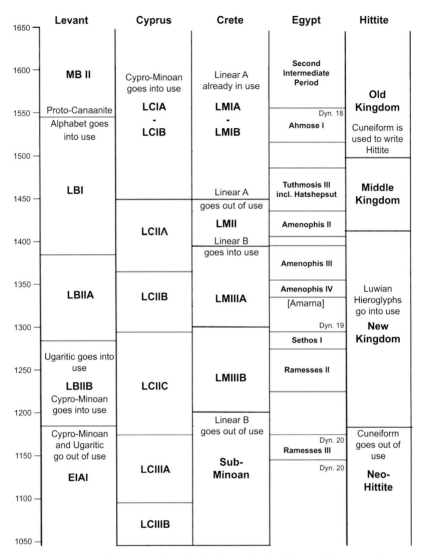

Figure 3 Approximate synchronized chronological chart of the Late Bronze
Age eastern Mediterranean.

processes involved in script transfer are rarely transparent in the historical
record and are highly variable. Script transfer can be conservative, wherein
the shapes, sounds, and document forms of one script are retained and applied to
writing a new language, or it can be selective. A script can be borrowed without
its document forms, and sign shapes can be borrowed without their sound
values, as was done by the inventor of the Cherokee syllabary, Sequoya, who
adopted shapes of some letters from the Roman alphabet to represent entirely
different sound values in his syllabary (Scancarelli, 1996). Script transfer can

also be combinatory, adapting signs from multiple scripts or even nonscript sources to create a new script.

The invention of the Cypro-Minoan script is believed to have involved script transfer from Linear A, one of the main scripts used on Crete and, to a lesser extent, the Cyclades from c. 1800–1450 BCE. Linear A was also the source script for the Linear B script used on Crete and the Greek mainland to write an early form of Greek called Mycenaean Greek from c. 1400–1190 BCE. Though Linear B and Cypro-Minoan were contemporaries, there is no evidence that the two scripts influenced one another at all. Some form of script transfer from Linear A to Cypro-Minoan is almost certainly assured, but its nature and extent are debated. Linear A may be one of several sources for Cypro-Minoan script signs. The small number of Cypro-Minoan texts from the 17th and 16th centuries, no more than four inscriptions and around fifty vessel texts, make reconstructing the circumstances of script transfer difficult.

Possible evidence for the setting of script transfer is a single-sign text on a discoid loom weight text from a small site in north-central Crete, Kalo Chorafi, dated broadly from 1800–1600 BCE. The discoid loom weight bears a single sign similar in shape to Cypro-Minoan script sign CM 061 (for a list of signs, see Section 2, Figure 7). The sign is definitely not a Linear A script sign, but neither is it incontrovertibly Cypro-Minoan. It is a sign of a simple shape that could also be a decorative motif. Until there is other evidence for Cypro-Minoan writing on Crete during the 17th century, the significance of the loom weight text is hard to interpret. Its presence could but does not necessarily indicate that Cypro-Minoan was invented on Crete. Alternatively, the sign could be a decoration or nonscript mark that later made its way into the Cypro-Minoan repertoire, or its similarity to a script sign could be coincidental.

The earliest certain Cypro-Minoan inscription, on a discoid loom weight from Enkomi, ##095 ENKO Apes 001, is datable to the LCI (see Figure 4). A second LCI inscription is on a clay tablet, also from Enkomi, ##001 ENKO Atab 001, but its script is not clearly related to Cypro-Minoan, only to (for an opposing view, Valério, 2018). Tablet ##001 has received a lot of attention from Cypro-Minoan scholars (see Steele, 2019, pp. 19–25 for an overview), but ##095 is just as, if not more, interesting. The object's function had previously been a matter of debate, with some proposing it is an economic label (Ferrara, 2012, pp. 53–56). Its identification as a discoid loom weight was confirmed only recently when the first study of LCI weaving technology was conducted by Giulia Muti in 2024.

Discoid loom weights were a technology associated with a particular form of textile production that began in Crete and spread throughout the Aegean, including to the Cyclades. Women likely played an important role in its spread, and therefore possibly that of Cypro-Minoan (Muti, 2024). Caution is needed.

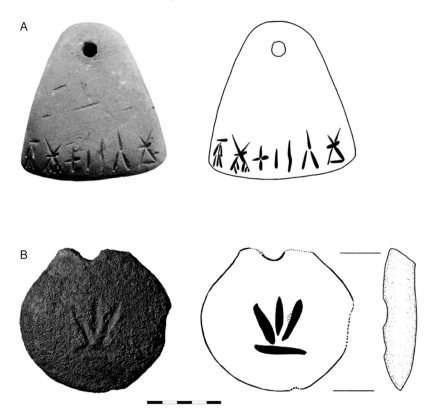

Figure 4 Comparison between inscribed discoid loom weights.
A. Loom weight ##095 Apes 001, h. 6.3, w. 7.2 cm. Note that the inscription is
upside down as pictured.

Photograph and drawing of ##095 by author, courtesy of the Cyprus Museum and the
Department of Antiquities, Cyprus.

B. Photograph and drawing of the Kalo Chorafi loom weight.

Courtesy of Anastasia Tzigounaki, Director of the Systematic Excavation of Kalo Chorafi,
Mylopotamos, Crete, Director of the Ephorate of Antiquities of Rethymno, and Dr. Artemis
Karnava.

though. Evidence for script transfer in weaving contexts is not quite there. The
two texts are on the same writing medium but different document forms. The
Kalo Chorafi loom weight carries a large text centered on the surface of the seal,
while the Enkomi weight carries its small text placed along its bottom edge.
Moreover, the Kalo Chorafi loom weight is not a certain Cypro-Minoan text.
The Enkomi inscription ##095 is the only Cypro-Minoan inscription on a loom
weight of any kind to date.

A potential candidate for the setting of script transfer could be the Cyclades,
where Linear A was written (and where discoid loom weights were used). A likely

Cypro-Minoan inscription has been identified as coming from the Cycladic island of Melos (Figure 2D). Its script was previously unidentified, but a recent Cypro-Minoan identification is compelling because a second Cypro-Minoan inscription on a vessel handle carries the same two-sign text (Figure 2C) and because the inscription fits the rules of representation of the Cypro-Minoan vessel handle document form (Donnelly, forthcoming). If the inscription is in fact written in Cypro-Minoan, then it is the only early inscription outside of Cyprus and the only one on a document form that continues into use past the period of script transfer. The strong associations between the vessel handle document form and trade could suggest that script transfer occurred in mercantile contexts (Hirschfeld, 2008), but there is scant evidence of a trade relationship between Cyprus and the Cyclades in the 17th and 16th centuries.

Without the discovery of new evidence, whether from Cyprus, Crete, or the Cyclades, the earliest period of Cypro-Minoan will remain poorly understood. For now, all that can be surmised is that the script underwent a long period of script diffusion, during which some elements of the Linear A script were adapted. Traders and/or individuals involved in textile production might have participated in the early spread of Cypro-Minoan, but the current evidence is simply too sparse for a clear picture to emerge.

1.2.2 The Amarna Period (c. 1350)

By the mid 14th century, during the so-called Amarna Period, Cyprus is a major player in overseas economic exchange. A cache of clay tablets, known as the Amarna Letters, discovered in the newly founded Egyptian capital of Akhetaten – modern Tell el-Amarna (whence Amarna Letters) – testifies to the economic prowess and integrated overseas economy of the eastern Mediterranean from roughly around 1360–1330 BCE. Written in the cuneiform script, these tablets mainly record the Akkadian language, which was being used as a diplomatic *lingua franca* (the classic translations are found in Moran, 2000).

Cyprus is a correspondent in the Amarna Letters. It is given the place name "Alashiya." Petrographic testing conducted on clay from the Amarna Tablets from Alashiya finds a good source for the clay in the southwest of Cyprus (Goren et al., 2004). Nevertheless, no cuneiform inscriptions have been found on Cyprus aside from some short, rote texts on cylinder seals. The existence of the Alashiya letters indicates that someone(s) on Cyprus had some formal cuneiform scribal training in how to write Akkadian, but current evidence suggests cuneiform was not widely used on Cyprus. Meanwhile, the use of Cypro-Minoan was slowly gaining steam and, despite fewer than twenty Cypro-Minoan inscriptions dating to the 14th century, would have been the dominant script used on the island.

The Amarna Letters document the economic and diplomatic maneuvering of the major players in the Late Bronze Age Mediterranean and Near East (see Figure 5). The major players were ruled by "Great Kings" (LUGAL.GAL in cuneiform) who refer to one another as metaphorical "brothers," distinguished by the term of address they use for their vassals, "son." An economic hierarchy of the Late Bronze Age in the 14th century has been reconstructed through a study of how the kings address one another and their subordinates. The Great Kings are the king of the Hittites in Anatolia, whose empire is at its height during the Amarna period, the king of the Land of Mitanni in northern Syria (associated with the Hurrian language), a once-proud empire on its last legs, the pharaoh of Egypt, and, more peripheral for our purposes, the kings of Assyria and Babylon. The kings of cities on the Levantine coasts, including the city of Ugarit in northern Syria, where Cypro-Minoan texts would later be written, all had vassal or "son" status. The palatial centers of Mycenaean Greece, where Linear B was written, were not mentioned.

Scholars frequently omit Cyprus from the list of Great Kings, but Cyprus's status as diplomatic equal with Egypt is clear (Humphrey, 2022). The king of Cyprus and the pharaoh call one another "brother," the form of address that was restricted to the Great Kings. Cyprus's equal diplomatic footing can be further intimated from the attitude and veiled insults – *the shade* – its king throws at the pharaoh, the likes of which subordinate kings would hardly dare. Yet the high diplomatic status of Cyprus and its king in the Amarna letters is belied by the material remains on Cyprus, where archaeological evidence for a king and a politically unified state is missing.

Many but not all archaeologists believe that 14th-century Cyprus was not a unified political entity but a "heterarchy" comprised of cities of relatively equal wealth and power, which each controlled its own hinterland (Peltenberg and Iacovou, 2012). Enkomi was one such city. What allowed Cyprus to rub proverbial elbows with the Great Kings was its vast copper reserves, which were being exploited to their fullest extent, and its traders, who played the role of middlemen between Mycenaean Greece to its west and the Levant and Egypt, circulating metals, oils, and wine (among other things). However this trade was conducted, it was likely not at the behest of a single centralized state with a king at its top (for an opposing view, Knapp, 2008, pp. 324–341). There is no royal iconography or architectural evidence of a single, centralized administrative and distributive center. Who the "king" of Cyprus was, whether he was a representative of one city or elected by all the cities to represent their interests in diplomatic correspondence, is a matter of continued academic debate.

The "internationalism" of the Amarna period increasingly gave way, in the early 13th century, to wars between the Hittites and Egyptians and general

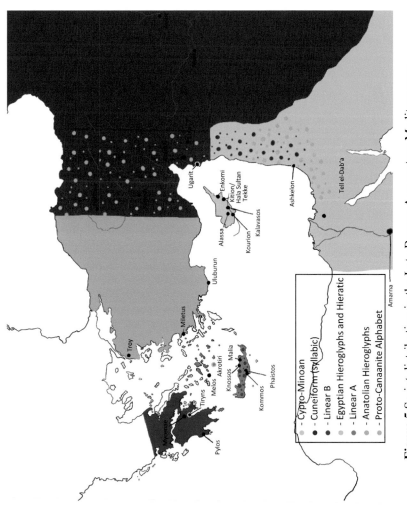

Figure 5 Script distribution in the Late Bronze Age eastern Mediterranean.

instability (for a summary, see Cline, 2021). One source of instability must have been the climate, which was aridifying at a swift pace. Another was intensified attacks by the so-called Sea Peoples, a group of marauding pirates straight from central casting. Despite their fantastical element, the Sea Peoples are noted in Egyptian, Hittite, and Ugaritic literary sources as a genuine destructive force. Scholars today paint the Sea Peoples variously as climate refugees or economic opportunists taking advantage of an unstable economic system. By the end of the 13th century and beginning of the 12th, the instability culminates in the so-called collapse of the major Amarna players, either through destruction or political weakening – except for Cyprus.

1.2.3 Before, during, and after the "Collapse" (c. 1250–1050)

The peak of Cypro-Minoan script use coincides with the so-called collapse period, better conceived of as a period of transition, in which large-scale, state-backed globalization was replaced by the small-scale but far-reaching independent trade networks like the ones writers of Cypro-Minoan participated in before and then during and after the collapse (Sherratt, 2003). In the Aegean, the major Mycenaean administrative centers of Mycenae and Pylos were destroyed and never used again. Same for the Hittite capital Hattuša and its vassal kingdom of Ugarit. Egypt sees the loss of its colonial empire and the division of the country into two parts, northern and southern.

What these places have in common is their reliance on centralized administration. The more decentralized, mercantile societies like Cyprus, and perhaps also Byblos and Sidon on coastal Lebanon or the traders of Ura on the Anatolian coast of Cilicia, could tap into far-reaching mercantile networks to maintain or create wealth. The breakdown of centralized administered states was accompanied by the loss or atrophy of the region's administrative scripts, namely cuneiform and Linear B. Some scripts were wiped from the pages of history until looting and archaeological investigation in the 19th century CE brought them back to light. One such script is Linear B, which went out of use completely and suddenly with the destruction of the Mycenaean palaces c. 1190 BCE. When Linear B was rediscovered in the late 19th century, no one knew that it was used to record the Greek language until its decipherment a half-century later in 1952 (for a wonderful video summary, www.youtube.com/watch?v=iePEw_cHp8s). Another is the alphabetic cuneiform script of Ugarit, a locally invented, short-lived script (c. 1250–1180) that went out of use so completely that its existence was wholly forgotten until its rediscovery and decipherment in the 20th century.

An equal but opposite effect was seen in the scripts of mercantile societies, which eventually blossomed after a lag of a century or two. In Anatolia, the local Luwian hieroglyphic script survived the collapse only to resurface as one of main scripts of the Neo-Hittite empires of the Iron Age in the 10th century BCE. But Luwian hieroglyphic inscriptions from the 12–10th centuries are few and far between (Hawkins, 2024). On the Levantine coast, the precursor to the Phoenician alphabet had been used since at least the 16th century, but inscriptions come in dribs and drabs until the end of the 11th century (Rollston, 2010). Only then did its use steadily increase until it gained enough steam to be adapted to write Greek, Etruscan, and Latin, becoming a template for our own alphabet. Of these scripts, only Cypro-Minoan is well documented during the late 13th and well into the 12th century. It therefore can serve as a proxy for thinking about how the scripts belonging to the other mercantile societies may have been transmitted in the absence of centralized administration.

Throughout the shifting landscape of the 12th century, Cyprus retains its wealth, conducts overseas trade, and exploits its copper resources, but it also undergoes changes. Some cities were abandoned while others underwent restructuring, like Enkomi, which centralized its copper workshops and revamped its sanctuaries. Sometime just before the destruction of Ugarit c. 1180, the king of Ugarit addresses letters to the "king of Alashiya," a certain Kušmešuša (the only Cypriot king whose name has been recorded), by calling him "my father," indicating that Cyprus and its king had a higher status than the king of the important port city (Singer, 1999, pp. 719–720). As ever, though, the island's political organization remains opaque, and there is little to no archaeological evidence for a unified state or a king.

The Cypro-Minoan script sees its furthest geographic extension during the collapse period. It was written locally in small amounts at Ugarit, just prior to its c. 1180 destruction, then at Tiryns in Greece just before and after the collapse of the Mycenaean palatial centers perhaps a decade earlier c. 1190. Short Cypro-Minoan inscriptions (which could have theoretically been written anywhere) are found on shipwrecks off the Anatolian and Levantine coasts. In the later 12th century, a single Cypro-Minoan inscription written on a northern Levantine vessel makes its way to Ashkelon in the southern Levant.

The use of Cypro-Minoan at Ugarit corresponds to the period of peak usage of the local alphabetic cuneiform script, Ugaritic (c. 1250–1180). The city was a major node in overseas and overland trade, an unhappy vassal of the Hittite kingdom of Anatolia. Texts written in at least five different scripts and nine different languages are found at the site, a testament to its connectivity and vitality (Boyes, 2021). Enkomi and Ugarit, facing one another a short one-day's sail across the sea, had close cultural, economic, and even political ties. Yet in other ways the two cities are culturally distinct in their political structures and their main local scripts (and probably languages).

The close relationship between Ugarit and Cyprus raises interesting questions about how and why we find Cypro-Minoan texts in Ugarit. As discussed in Section 4, traders may have been integral to the dissemination and local production of Cypro-Minoan texts. At Ugarit, traders conducted trade both in their own names and in the names of the king or queen of Ugarit. Exactly how and on whose behalf Cypriot traders worked is not something we currently understand, but it is conceivable that the commercial initiative afforded to Ugaritian traders was echoed across the sea at Enkomi. The ability of individuals to move goods and strike deals on their own behalf could explain how traders from Ugarit and Cyprus became intimately acquainted enough to share writing practices and how writers of Cypro-Minoan were able to retain use of their script during the collapse that saw Ugarit destroyed.

1.3 What Comes Next

The explosion of Cypro-Minoan writing during and after the collapse period provides a perfect case study for thinking about how and why writing is transmitted outside of scribal school or administrative settings. Very few Cypro-Minoan document forms were administrative. Instead, they fall into two basic types, mercantile document forms and insular document forms. Mercantile document forms comprise texts written on objects frequently traded overseas, and insular document forms semistandardized texts on objects found mostly within Cyprus. What they have in common is that their document forms are almost always unique or creatively adapted in Cyprus from abroad and exhibit less standardization than the products of scribal and administrative counterparts. The variation within and across mercantile and insular document forms suggests that Cypro-Minoan writers transmitted knowledge about how to write in a variety of settings and that instruction in writing was less rule-bound than in contemporary scribal and administrative writing settings. Mercantile document forms, especially, would have traveled widely and been handled by numerous people with different levels of reading and writing comprehension. In such settings, who was writing for whom and to what end? If writing was not produced for purposes of administration and not as part of a scribal curriculum, then why did writers of Cypro-Minoan write?

The writers of Cypro-Minoan and their script are the stars of this Element. The variation and creativity exhibited in the material features of Cypro-Minoan document forms provide evidence for their lives, even as their script remains undeciphered. Section 2 discusses the prospect of decipherment and explains how the same variation that makes the script such an interesting object of study impedes its decipherment. Section 3 examines the history of Cypro-Minoan scholarship, especially its intersection with the island's colonial past. It questions the extent to which any study of the past can be separated from the social and political attitudes of the scholar. Sections 4 and 5 take a deep dive into mercantile and insular document forms, respectively, studying them for clues about who their writers were, whom they wrote for, and why. Even though Cypro-Minoan remains and for the foreseeable future likely will remain undeciphered, the material features of its texts still communicate with us.

2 Approaches to Decipherment

Cypro-Minoan presents scholars with one clear advantage in decipherment attempts but many more obstacles. The clear advantage in decipherment is that a significant portion of Cypro-Minoan signs were adopted from Linear A, and it is therefore theoretically possible to reconstruct at least some of the sound values of the signs borrowed from that script. The disadvantages are myriad. Successful decipherment efforts require one or all of the following parameters to be met: (1) the presence of a bilingual; (2) the script records a known language; or (3) the existence of long texts and/or many texts, sufficient to build an accurate inventory of signs (a "signary") and word lists. Cypro-Minoan offers scholars none of the above. To be met, parameter 1 will require fortuitous new discoveries. Parameter 2 is outside of anyone's control. Only parameter 3 leaves some room for hope. Even though Cypro-Minoan has produced very few inscriptions of length, new technologies allow scholars to do more with less data. They can assist in the construction of a more accurate signary and in computational analysis that extracts more patterns from less information.

2.1 Script, Language, and Decipherment

Decipherment consists of two conceptually separable but often practically intertwined stages: (1) the reading stage, in which the sound values for the unknown signs are ascertained, and (2) the language identification stage, in which the sound values are "tried on" to see if they fit the linguistic patterns belonging to any known languages. This "reading" is not like reading in the everyday sense of the term where a text is read for its meaning. Rather, reading in the context of decipherment consists only of reading the sound values of script signs. The two stages of decipherment correspond to the two different facets of writing: (1) script, the written communication mode, and (2) language, the spoken communication mode recorded by the script.

Recognizing the differences between script and language is key to understanding decipherment processes. Recalling the example of the Roman alphabet discussed in Section 1, a single script can be used to record a myriad of languages. Likewise, a single language can be recorded by a variety of scripts. Take, for instance, Greek. The first known script to record the Greek language was the Linear B script, the contemporary relative of Cypro-Minoan mentioned in Section 1. Several centuries after the use of Linear B ceased along with the collapse of the Mycenaean palatial centers, the Phoenician alphabet was adapted to write Greek. That script eventually evolved into the Greek script still used today. At different points in its history, the Greek language has been written in the Hebrew script by Jews living in Greek-speaking lands and in the Arabic script by Greek speakers living in predominantly Turkish-speaking areas in the Ottoman empire (Stroebel, 2017).

The separable properties of script and language mean that decipherers can apply different techniques to "read" the script and decode its sound values and to "identify" its underlying language. A partial decipherment, where sound values can be read but the language remains unidentified, is a possible outcome of decipherment efforts. For instance, linguists have demonstrated the likelihood that the sound values of the core Linear A signs in script transfer to Linear B were borrowed along with the shapes of the script signs. It is therefore possible to "read" Linear A using Linear B sound values even as the language(s) recorded by the Linear A script remain unidentified. In such cases, we can say that a script is partially deciphered. The mix-and-match nature of scripts and languages means that decipherers should be open to the possibility that Cypro-Minoan could record multiple, even unrelated languages and that the script may one day be readable but remain undeciphered.

2.1.1 Verifying Decipherment

For a full and successful decipherment, readings of proposed sound values and language identification must be verifiable. Proposed sound values should be tested and applied to multiple documents, not just one. Language identification cannot rest solely on the identification of individual words in a given language but also on grammar. In cases of scripts that record known languages, decipherments are relatively easy to verify. For instance, Michael Ventris suspected that his decipherment was successful when he was able to read the word *tripod* on a Linear B tablet. The word *tripod* is comprised of strong Greek roots (*tria* = three, *pous* = foot) and appeared on the tablet next to a drawing of a three-footed vessel. But it was not until his proposed readings for the signs yielded results matching Greek grammar that the decipherment was generally accepted. The true test of decipherment is grammar, not the ability to read individual words.

Grammar encompasses the way that different words or parts of words (morphemes) relate to one another in a sentence. Often, the position of words in a sentence and the form of words change depending on their grammatical role. Take, for instance, the changes in the simple sentences, "I give you a hot dog" and "you gave me the hot dog": I/me changes forms based on its role in the sentence, give/gave changes according to tense, and the word "you," though remaining unchanged in form, moves word position as its role changes. Grammatical features are a language's fingerprint, distinguishing it from other languages even as certain features are inevitably shared with them.

Grammar is a much more reliable indicator of language identification than individual words. Michael Ventris's identification of *tripod* is a case in point. The etymology of the word is certainly Greek, but it is a word that has been inherited into English, Italian, and French and could appear in texts recording any of those languages. Names can likewise be misleading. My first name has a clear Greek etymology, but my native language is English, and I have no familial roots in Greece. Individual words are not good indicators of the language recorded by a script, but grammar is.

Verification of decipherment requires replication of results across multiple documents. It is precisely on this count that Cypro-Minoan presents the most impediments. Very few texts are long enough to exhibit complex grammar: only six inscriptions are longer than 100 words (##097–098, ##207–209, ##215), which is an impediment to decipherment itself, and the longer texts, for reasons discussed in Section 2.3, might record different languages from one another. If this is indeed the case, then not only is the prospect of decipherment quite low but so is the ability to verify a decipherment.

2.1.2 What We Know about Cypro-Minoan

A first step to decipherment is determining the type of script (is it an alphabet? a syllabary?) and the number and nature of sounds in the script. The type of script can usually be identified by counting the number of unique signs it exhibits. Alphabets usually have the fewest number of signs (fewer than 50), syllabaries between 50 and 100 signs, and logographic writing systems hundreds. Insights into phonology, the number and nature of sounds in a language, are much more difficult to realize. One almost always needs to know additional information about the script, such as the languages spoken in and around its home region or if it is related to scripts with known sound values. In that case, one can make educated guesses about the script's phonology, that is, the number and types of sounds it records. The field of linguistic typology, which aims to discover general tendencies in how languages work, can provide general guidelines for testing hypotheses but is not always a reliable tool because of the many exceptions that individual languages present.

In the case of Cypro-Minoan, the identification of the script as a syllabary has been inferred from a comparison to the related Linear A and Cypro-Syllabic scripts. Linear A provides the source for anywhere from twelve to thirty of Cypro-Minoan's around ninety signs (see Figure 7), some of whose sound values are known through comparison to Linear B. Cypro-Syllabic is the "daughter" script of Cypro-Minoan, used c. 1000–300 BCE. Cypro-Syllabic adapted a significant portion of Cypro-Minoan sign shapes in its script transfer from Cypro-Minoan, reducing the number of signs to fifty-five. It is not clear whether Cypro-Syllabic inherited the sound values of Cypro-Minoan except in a handful of cases. The Cypro-Syllabic script was used to record at least two languages. The first is the main language recorded in Cypro-Syllabic inscriptions, Greek, which was widely spoken on Iron Age Cyprus, and the second an unknown language or languages, recorded on fewer than thirty inscriptions, most from the 5th and 4th centuries BCE, referred to as Eteocypriot, supposedly a language indigenous to Cyprus (Egetmeyer, 2010). Comparing Cypro-Minoan to Linear A and Cypro-Syllabic reveals some basic insights but has not led to the ability to read most Cypro-Minoan signs nor to identify its underlying language(s).

Comparison of Cypro-Minoan to Linear A and Cypro-Syllabic suggest that it is a syllabary that records vowel signs and open syllabic signs (i.e., *ba*, *pa*, *ra*, and so on). Secure sound values for nine to eleven signs are obtained by comparing the sound values of signs with the same shape across Cypro-Minoan, Linear A/B, and Cypro-Syllabic. The nine to eleven signs suggest that Cypro-Minoan has at least four vowel sounds, *a*, *e*, *i*, and *o*, and the following consonants, *-s*, *t/d*, *r/l*, and *-p*. Attempts to derive new information from comparisons across the three scripts are common but often not successful. Miguel Valério, as recently as 2016, advanced a more accurate method of sign-shape comparison, basing his comparison not on the abstract drawings of sign shapes (sometimes called "normalized" drawings), as his predecessors had done, but on the actual examples of sign shapes in inscriptions. Despite his improvement to the comparative method, his interscript comparisons result in readings for only about thirty signs, many of which are still highly contested, sometimes requiring signs to be flipped upside down, turned around, or otherwise reimagined to produce shape matches. The insights into the script gained by comparisons to Linear A and Cypro-Syllabic are limited.

Only a single feature of grammar has been identified with any degree of certainty: the ending *-Co-ti* (C = consonant of any value), which is believed to indicate a genitive or dative ("belonging to" or "to/for" X). The *-Co-ti* feature has been identified through comparison to bilingual Greek–Eteocypriot Cypro-Syllabic inscriptions (Masson, 1971, p. 26). Although the Eteocypriot language remains unidentified, when its signs are read with and compared to the Greek words in the bilingual inscriptions, it is apparent that the *-Co-ti* affix indicates a genitive or dative, often with an inscription dedicated "to/for" or "belonging to" a name ending in *-Co-ti*. Luckily, the Cypro-Syllabic *ti* sign has the same shape and sound value as the Linear A sign for *ti*. It is therefore likely that the Cypro-Minoan sign of the same shape, CM 023, has the same *ti* sound value. CM 023 appears frequently in word-final position in Cypro-Minoan inscriptions. Although this is often taken as proof that the Cypro-Minoan inscriptions that show possible *-Co-ti* endings and Eteocypriot record the same language, other explanations are possible. It may be the case that a *Co-ti* feature was shared by two different languages because of their proximity, a linguistic process called areal diffusion, or through frequent contact.

2.2 Computational Approaches, New Technologies, and Signaries

2.2.1 Computational Approaches

Perhaps the most important prerequisite for decipherment is the accurate identification of unique signs and their range of sign variants. Accurate sign identification is necessary for getting a true count of the total number of signs in a script, for identifying how a sign behaves in words (i.e., its preferred word position), and for identifying features of the underlying language's grammar. The shape of individual script signs can vary considerably and for many reasons: personal whimsy, physical limitations, regional differences in scribal training, or simply because training in a certain script does not impose uniformity on its writers. Different fonts illustrate how the shapes of signs **change considerably** from font to font. One of the main tasks in decipherment is to determine if signs of similar shape are the same sign with same sound value, that is, variants of the same unique sign, or if they are different unique signs with their own sound values. Is the serifed and dotted "i" of Times New Roman the same sign as the simplified line i with an acute mark from Papyrus as the dotted line of i Comic Sans? Comparing only the shapes of signs to identify whether they are unique signs or variants of one another can be misleading. A much more reliable method is to observe how a sign behaves, its preferred word position, the signs it frequently appears next to, and repeated sign sequences in which it appears.

Computational analysis is one of most important tools that decipherers have for constructing a sign's behavioral profile. The pioneer of computational analysis in the decipherment of Aegean scripts, working without a computer, is the American scholar Alice E. Kober (1906–1950), whose work was instrumental in Michael Ventris's eventual decipherment of Linear B. Instead of trying to "read" Linear B by guessing sound values, Kober assembled and analyzed lists of Linear B words to observe sign behavior (see Figure 6). Due to paper shortages in World War II, Kober assembled word lists on homemade index cards cut from scrap paper and stored in cigarette cartons (Fox 2013). On her index cards, she catalogued how many times each sign appeared, its preferred word position, which signs it appeared next to, lists of repeated sign sequences, and more, conducting a decades-long, long-form computational analysis of sign frequency and word position, unaided by computers.

Positional analysis of signs and permutations of repeated sign sequences are potent tools for identifying individual signs and their variants. Imagine you are an alien beamed down to earth and given a code to decipher. The code consists of two sets of numbers, 1352, 8901352, 13526, 1752, and *1352, 8901352, 13526, 1752*. Being an alien, you have never seen numbers before. One of your first steps toward decipherment will be to determine if the codes are identical. Looking at the shapes of the signs alone will lead you down a wrong path. The first sign in each set, "1 and *1*," for instance, have similarities and differences in their shape which may or may not be meaningful. Comparing how the two signs behave in each set of code is simpler and more conclusive: Both signs appear frequently in word-initial position, are often followed by sign 3, and recur in a repeated sign sequence 1352. It is therefore highly likely that 1 and *1* are variants of the same unique sign.

Next, you might try to identify the encoded language by looking for grammatical features recorded in the code, 1352, 8901352, 13526, 1752, and comparing them to known languages. A simple computational analysis would show that "1352" is a repeated sequence that can take a prefix (890), a suffix (6), and an internal modification (1352 v. 1752) called an *ablaut*. The language recoded in the code can thus be narrowed down to languages with suffixes, prefixes, and ablauts, such as Germanic languages. In fact, that's what the code records: the English words "give," "forgive," "given," and "gave." Kober used a similar process in her study of Linear B, identifying a grammatical element called declension in sets of three repeated sign sequences that showed internal and word-final permutations, known today as "Kober's triplets" (see Figure 6). Although Kober was not able to use this information to decipher the script herself, Kober's triplets were instrumental in Michael Ventris's realization that Linear B records Mycenaean Greek.

Cypro-Minoan has proven resistant to traditional computational analysis approaches like Kober's. The inscriptions are simply too short and too few to ascertain statistically significant information about each sign's preferred word

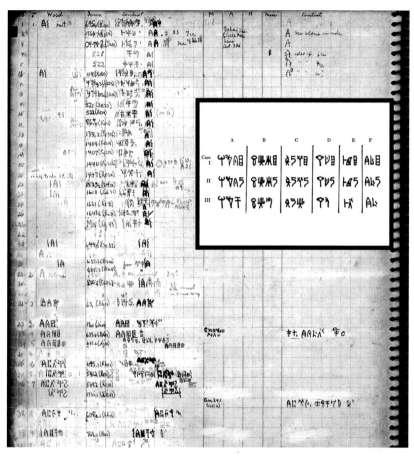

Figure 6 Image from Alice E. Kober's *Word List* notebook with "Kober's triplets" inset in black.

Notebook image courtesy of the Program of Aegean Scripts and Prehistory, University of Texas, Austin.

position. There are also very few repeated sign sequences and even fewer with permutations. New technologies may prove instrumental in providing a way forward. Advances in statistical modeling can assist, among other things, in determining the positional frequencies of infrequently attested signs with a degree of statistical significance unreachable using older methods. Christina Skelton, in collaboration with a team of computer scientists from the University of California San Diego, for instance, refined computational methods to produce behavior profiles for Cypro-Minoan signs across all inscriptions (Skelton et al., 2022). Skelton and her team concluded that individual signs had different positional frequency across different inscriptions, a result that they interpreted to mean either that different inscriptions recorded different languages or different topics/genres of documents (more on that in Section 2.3).

Advances in artificial intelligence technologies (AI), such as deep learning and neural networks, have made great strides in the realms of translation and language identification using less and less input data. Deep-learning-based neural networks tasked with identifying the sound values of unknown signs recording known languages have been successful, including one tasked with identifying the underlying language of Linear B (for an overview, Ferrara and Tamburini, 2022). A team of script scholars and computer scientists in Italy has trained neural network technologies to analyze and identify Cypro-Minoan sign shapes (Corazza et al., 2022). The fields of Machine Translation (MT) and Natural Language Processing (NLP) have developed automatic translation tools to target translations for languages with small datasets and without known language data inputs. Any of these technologies, or a combination thereof, might one day be successfully applied to attempts to decipher Cypro-Minoan. For any of these new computational methods to one day be successful, however, the most important task is for scholars of Cypro-Minoan to develop as accurate a signary as possible.

2.2.2 Signaries

Computational analysis of sign frequency and position can only be as accurate as its data. The greatest barrier to Cypro-Minoan decipherment efforts at present is the lack of an agreed-upon inventory of signs, or "signary." There is no agreement on the number of Cypro-Minoan signs because there is no agreement on which signs are unique and which are variants. Historically, the greatest impediment to the creation of an accurate signary was the inability of scholars to distinguish between script and nonscript signs. Today, the greatest difficulty is figuring out how to distinguish unique signs and their variants without the aid of traditional computational analysis.

Distinguishing script from nonscript signs was difficult for early scholars of Cypro-Minoan because the earliest inscriptions were few and short. As we know now, single-sign texts contain an assortment of script and nonscript signs, but for much of the history of Cypro-Minoan there was no method for distinguishing script from nonscript signs. The earliest signaries simply aggregated lists of every sign depicted on every known text. The result was that they often included what are today known to be nonscript signs.

The first method for distinguishing script from nonscript signs was developed by the American archaeologist and wartime spy John Franklin Daniel, who had been the lead excavator at the site of Episkopi-Bamboula in the 1930s, where his team discovered over eighty Cypro-Minoan texts, most of them single-sign texts on vessels, tripling the total number of Cypro-Minoan texts (Daniel, 1941). Faced with so many new texts, Daniel sought to impose order on a chaotic dataset. He developed a hierarchical assessment for determining whether a sign was a script sign or not. He counted a sign as a script sign with confidence, first, if it appeared in a multisign inscription, which he believed guaranteed that the sign was used to spell a word and hence to record language; second, with less confidence, if a sign with the same shape was attested in another Aegean script (such as Linear A); and third, with even less confidence, if the sign frequently recurred on single-sign texts.

After World War II, when a trove of longer inscriptions was unearthed, Daniel's method for identifying script signs was no longer needed. Scholars simply could count a sign as a script sign if it appears in a multisign inscription. Since then, scholars have tried and failed to develop signaries using computational approaches based on positional frequencies and repeated sign sequences. One of the more ambitious approaches to the signary, of late, was taken by Miguel Valério, who combined computational analysis with cross-script comparisons of Cypro-Minoan signs with Linear A and Cypro-Syllabic. Valério's signary produced a wide-ranging number of possible signs, fifty-seven on the low end and seventy on the high end, showing both the benefits and limitations of more traditional approaches to Cypro-Minoan (Valério, 2016, pp. 166–171, 442).

A novel approach to the signary was taken by Martina Polig, who created a signary based on an analysis of sign shape alone (Polig and Donnelly, 2022, see Figure 7). Sign shape has not historically been regarded a useful unit of analysis in decipherment (see the discussion of "1 vs. l"), but Polig harnessed the advantages provided by new technologies to create an accurate dataset analyzable on a greater scale than before. Using structured-light scanning technology, she created millimeter-accurate 3D models that recorded the shape of every undamaged sign from every available Cypro-Minoan inscription, and then she catalogued, measured, and compared each sign, which enabled her to observe "rules" according to which sign variants were produced from unique signs.

The result is an eighty-nine-sign signary, called an "integrated signary" because it presents the unique signs along with their variants. It is the signary used throughout this Element when referring to signs. In Cypro-Minoan studies, it is common to refer to signs by their number in the signary since their sound values are not known. The numbers Polig chose for her signs adhere as closely as possible to the numbering system that was first put into place by Émilia Masson in the 1970s and which was followed, with modifications, in subsequent signaries (for a history of Cypro-Minoan signaries, see Polig and Donnelly, 2022). I have chosen to present the integrated signary here because it is the only

Integrated CM signary with variants

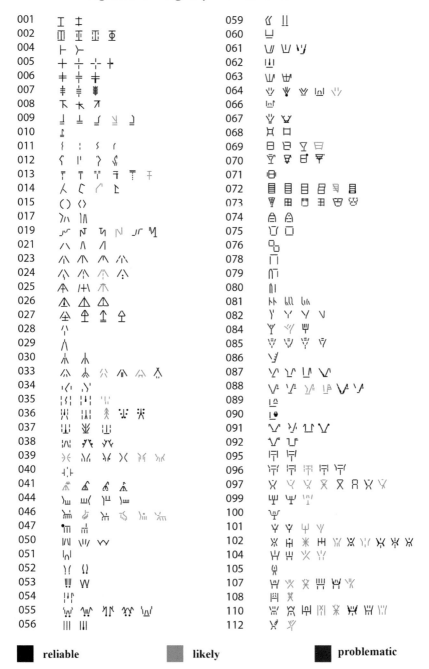

reliable   likely   problematic

Figure 7 Polig and Donnelly's "integrated signary."

Image courtesy of Polig and Donnelly, 2022.

signary built from accurate images of the whole spectrum of Cypro-Minoan inscriptions and the only one to represent sign variants alongside unique signs. It shows the wide variation of Cypro-Minoan sign shapes in all its glory.

2.3 Cypro-Minoan Decipherment Attempts

The earliest Cypro-Minoan decipherment attempts were quite unsophisticated, like that of Swedish scholar Axel Persson, writing in 1937, who simply guessed which language the script belonged to (Greek) and then tried with sound values borrowed from Cypro-Syllabic and his own imagination to produce readings of Greek words (Persson, 1937). Persson had the disadvantage that he had little recourse to good data from which to attempt a decipherment. In 1937, Linear B was still undeciphered and the number of Cypro-Minoan inscriptions fewer than fifty.

More recently, aspiring Cypro-Minoan decipherers have restricted their efforts to specific inscriptions or sets of inscriptions. Three texts/sets of texts in particular have been the subject of language-identification efforts: clay cylinder ##097 ENKO Arou 001 from Enkomi, clay tablet ##215 RASH Atab 004 from Ugarit, and the three clay tablets from Enkomi with uniform paleography (##207–209 ENKO Atab 002–4). These texts have been singled out for decipherment because they are each longer than 100 signs, that is, long enough to potentially betray elements of grammar. Certain suggestions recur: (1) clay cylinder ##097 records an indigenous language, a precursor to Eteocypriot; (2) tablet ##215 from Ugarit records a Semitic language; and (3) Enkomi clay tablets ##207–209 record Hurrian. At first blush, it might seem promising that the same proposals are made again and again, but none of the suggested readings and language identifications is applied across multiple inscriptions with consistent, positive results in the form of identified grammar. If a scholar truly has made a partial decipherment and uncovered the correct sound values of Cypro-Minoan signs, the sound values can only be verified if and when they yield readings across multiple inscriptions.

The decipherment efforts centered on Ugarit tablet ##215, widely considered to be a list because of its formatting, are a case in point (see Figure 8). A focal point of the Semitic-language identifications is the interpretation of the two-sign sequence, 051–028, which repeats throughout the inscription. It has been interpreted to record a Semitic word for "son," in the common Semitic formula "X son of X" (Masson, 1974; Nahm, 1981; Valério, 2016, pp. 353–396). But the proposals are not consistent with one another in the sound values they assign or languages they propose. Nahm reads the sequence 051–028 as *pi-ru* (Aramaic; *br*), Masson *pi-nu* (Ugaritic; *binu*), and Valério *pi-lu* (Ugaritic; *binu*). The inconsistencies noted here

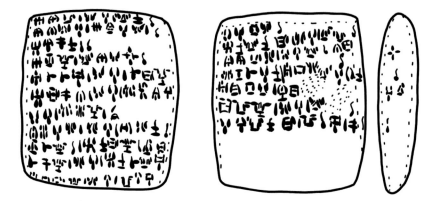

Figure 8 Illustration of the material features of Ugarit tablet, ##215
RASH Atab 004; h 5.8, w, 6.8 cm. Should not be regarded as an authoritative
depiction of sign variants.

Drawing by author based on photographs in Ferrara, 2012.

are not intended to invalidate these proposals but to demonstrate the degree of
flexibility and interpretation that can be introduced into the language-identification
stage of decipherment. Another area of flexibility is introduced in the Semitic and
Hurrian names each proposed scholar to read in the text. The list of names
recorded at Ugarit alone comprises c. 2,600 names derived from multiple languages, many of uncertain pronunciation because Ugaritic does not record vowels
(Van Soldt, 1991). The chance of coincidental similarities between the proposed
sound values and over 1,000 names of flexible pronunciation is high. The flexibility introduced by language-identification proposals is why proposed decipherments of individual inscriptions need confirmation from other inscriptions.

Proposals that the Enkomi tablets record Hurrian, the most notable of which
is that of Émilia Masson, are not widely accepted because they show no clear
evidence of Hurrian grammar in the texts (Masson, 1974). They are illustrative,
however, of some of the difficulties of attempting language identification on
a language like Hurrian, which has significant structural differences compared
to both Indo-European (e.g. Greek) and Semitic languages. The differences in
phonemic inventory, and the fact that not all sound values are known, mean that
a potential decipherer has a wider degree of flexibility in interpreting sound
values than they might otherwise have. Moreover, Hurrian is an agglutinative
language, not an inflectional one like Indo-European and Semitic languages.
Unlike inflectional languages that permute affixes to change a word's meaning
(remember give, forgive, given), agglutinative languages add series of affixes. If
Cypro-Minoan records an agglutinative language or a language otherwise
structurally   different   from   Indo-European   and   Semitic   languages,

computational methods would have to be adapted to recognize the difference. Any Hurrian language identifications should be able to demonstrate an agglutinative grammar footprint in the inscriptions.

The identification of clay cylinder ##097 (see Figure 9) with an indigenous "Eteocypriot" language rests on a single feature, the *-Co-ti* ending discussed in Section 2.1 possibly shared between Cypro-Minoan and the less than thirty, significantly later Eteocypriot inscriptions (see, for instance, Janko, 2020). The shared feature is an element of grammar, but without corroborating elements of grammar common to both sets of inscriptions, it is impossible to say that the 13th-century cylinder and the much later Eteocypriot inscriptions record the same language. They could simply record two different languages that share a common feature – how, for instance, many participles in Greek and English share an "nd" affix or how many unrelated languages today borrow "Mr." as a title.

The most significant failing of these and similar claims of language identification is that they rest on the identification of individual words or names but not grammar. The identification of names is often a helpful first step in decipherment, as it was in the decipherment of the Egyptian scripts, for instance (Parkinson, 1999). But unlike like the thousands upon thousands of texts written in Egyptian hieroglyphs and hieratic, Cypro-Minoan has only six texts longer than 100 words. It is therefore much more difficult to verify if a proposed set of sound values is reasonable or if a successful decipherment has occurred. Name or word identifications can be the result of coincidence, creating the illusion of language identification. It may also be the case that the language in which a name is recorded is different than the language of the text

Figure 9 Clay cylinder ##097 ENKO Arou 001; h. 6.3, w. 7.3 cm. Note CM 023 at the end of words on lines 1, 2, and 3 (L1, L2, L3).

Photograph courtesy of the Program in Aegean Scripts and Prehistory, University of Texas, Austin. Drawing by author from 3D model, courtesy of Martina Polig.

(see, for instance, the present author's very Greek first name, first recorded in the Mycenaean Linear B tablets as *ke-sa-da-ra*). Grammar, by contrast, is complex, patterned, and language-specific. It is therefore less likely that assigned sound values could randomly mimic its features.

Enkomi clay cylinder ##097 is illustrative of another problem that the longer Cypro-Minoan inscriptions present: the nagging feeling that they do not all record the same languages as one another. ##097 is either missing the most common sign in Cypro-Minoan, CM 102, which occurs eighty-two times, or employs a unique variant of it (Figure 7, CM 102 Variant 7). CM 102 has an overwhelming preference for word-initial position (98.8% of all attestations; Valério, 2016, p. 308, table 4.4). The exception is on this cylinder, if its unique sign is in fact a variant of CM 102. These oddities, and others, could indicate that the cylinder records a different language or, if not a different language, a different topic or genre than the other long inscriptions.

Distinguishing whether a document might record different languages versus different topics can be more difficult than you might at first think, especially when the documents in question are short. A grocery list, for instance, is a type of text that contains very little grammar but series of words, sometimes derived from a wide variety of languages: zucchini (Italian), okra (Igbo), cumin (Akkadian, but already attested in Mycenaean Linear B), tomato (Nahuatl) . . . and that's just lunch! Compare that to an office memo, which will have extensive grammar and a formal register of highfalutin words with Greek and Latin etymologies, "Dear colleagues, I hereby encourage microwave operators to sterilize the machine after every usage," to a text message exchanged between friends replete wth shorthand spellngs, limited punctuation n lotsa diff emoji ☺ ☹ :p n stckrs. It may well be the case that the perceived differences between the inscriptions result from the different topics they cover, not that they record different languages (Skelton et al., 2022).

The colonial history of Cyprus is entangled in the history of Cypro-Minoan scholarship and decipherment efforts. It helps explain, in part, why scholars from different countries, writing in different time periods, sought the language identifications they did. As much as scientists of any kind, including archaeologists and historians of writing, aim to develop theories and analyze data in an unbiased manner, lived experience always influences perceptions, as we will see again in Section 3. The history of Cypro-Minoan scholarship, then, is as much a modern history of Cyprus as an ancient one.

3 Defining a Script

3.1 Cypro-Minoan: The First Fifty Years of Its Discovery (1896–1950)

The stories scholars tell about the past, this one included, are consciously and unconsciously influenced by contemporary biases and anxieties. The study of Cypro-Minoan is a case in point. It is permeated by the colonial ideologies that buttressed Britain's colonization of the island and the counterideologies that defied it. Knowing something of Cyprus's colonial history and postcolonial present is key to understanding Cypro-Minoan scholarship.

Cypro-Minoan was discovered and initially studied in 1896 during the Protectorate period of British rule, 1878 to 1913, and accelerated when the British empire had formal control over the island, first as an annexed territory (1914–1924) and then as a Crown colony (down to 1960). The British administration encouraged the island's major religious groups, Greek-speaking Orthodox Christians and Turkish-speaking Muslims, to increasingly identify themselves in ethnic, linguistic, and national terms linked to their respective "motherlands" of Greece and Türkiye. After a brief period of independence (1960–1974) marked by internecine conflict culminating in the Turkish invasion in 1974, the Republic of Cyprus was officially divided along a United Nations Buffer Zone, the so-called Green Line. The northern third of the island was, and is still, occupied by Türkiye, and the southern two-thirds of the island is controlled by the Republic of Cyprus. As a result of fierce battles and forced migrations, Christian Greek Cypriots predominate in the Republic of Cyprus and Muslim Turkish Cypriots in the occupied territory, where they are becoming a minority after decades of Turkish state-supported migrations from the mainland. Today, Cypriots on both sides of the Green Line inhabit a range of identities from Cypriot, Greek-Cypriot, and Turkish-Cypriot, to Greek and Turkish no hyphen, not forgetting to mention the island's long-standing Maronite Christian, Armenian, and Lebanese populations and new Turkish populations, among others. Most Cypriot identities privilege religion and language as the primary indicators of ethnicity, a legacy of British colonial policy.

Archaeology was and is one arena where Cypriots contest their identity. During the colonial period, Greek Cypriots who called for rejecting British colonial rule and joining the Greek nation state (a political movement called *enosis*) appealed to archaeology to establish the island's Greek pedigree, the older the evidence the better. Turkish Cypriots, on the other hand, largely ignored the Bronze Age past, emphasizing instead Cyprus's multicultural medieval past and its centuries under Ottoman rule (Bounia et al., 2021). Consequently, Cypro-Minoan scholarship mostly records the interpretations of Greek Cypriot and European scholars, many part of the British colonial apparatus, while Turkish Cypriot perspectives are largely absent.

Throughout much of the history of Cypro-Minoan studies, European and Greek-Cypriot scholars alike were fixated on the ethnic origins of Cypro-Minoan writers. The obsession with ethnic origins was common in archaeological studies from the 19th and 20th centuries, falling out of fashion only in the past fifty years. According to this worldview, ethnicity was a geographically bound, immutable aspect of an individual or group's character (Jones, 1997). Different ethnic groups produced different material cultures, that is, different types of pottery, art, scripts, and so on, in accordance with their different ethnic traits. This worldview became part of the armature of colonialism. When used to justify British and French domination over the Levant and the Middle East, a colonial ideology known today as "Orientalism," it manifested in the assumption that Europeans were an ethnicity characterized by their industriousness, intelligence, and civilized character, and Levantines its opposite – lethargic, superstitious, backwards (for the classic text on orientalism, Said, 1978). There is absolutely no scientific basis to the idea that ethnicity is an immutable trait, quite the contrary, but the idea was so long-standing and so integral to the foundation of archaeology as an academic discipline that it leaves its insidious imprint on the study of Cypro-Minoan, even in the work of scholars who did not ascribe to it.

3.1.1 Earliest Discoveries

Cypro-Minoan can be seen as something of a Rorschach test of colonial ideologies. The origins of the script became a focal point for determining the "ethnic" character of the island's ancient and modern inhabitants. Depending on the political situation, European and Greek Cypriot scholars alike posited European (specifically Greek/Cretan), "Oriental," and sometimes indigenous Cypriot origins for the script. A template for a vacillating Cypriot identity was provided by its Iron Age past when its cities were split between Greek and Phoenician rule. Already in the 19th century, the many Phoenician inscriptions found on the island were taken to demonstrate the Levantine, "Oriental" ethnic character of the island's inhabitants. That conclusion was upended in the 1870s, however, when the British autodidact George Smith deciphered Cypro-Syllabic and demonstrated that most Cypro-Syllabic inscriptions record the Greek language.

Smith's decipherment impacted different communities in different ways. For many Greek Cypriots, the decipherment reinforced their sense of Greek ethnic identity. It also lent ideological backing to the *enosis* movement's fight to join the Greek nation state. Many European archaeologists, at least at first, welcomed Smith's decipherment as proof that writing on Cyprus was a European invention, another feather in their superior European caps. But exactly at the time *enosis* gained momentum in the 1940s and 1950s and posed a serious threat to colonial rule, as first noted by archaeologist Michael Given, they pivoted to the idea that writing on Cyprus was an "indigenous" tool (Given, 1998). The earliest discoveries of Cypro-Minoan and their subsequent interpretations were impacted by the broader political climate on the island at most every turn.

The first Cypro-Minoan texts, unearthed in the late 1890s by a privately funded British expedition to Cyprus, were short and single-sign texts on vessels and short inscriptions on clay balls. They contained no more than fifteen unique signs among them on fewer than thirty texts (Evans, 1909, p. 68). Despite their brevity and small number, all were interpreted as writing. Sir Arthur Evans, the British archaeologist who established the discipline of Aegean scripts and whose belief in the racial superiority of Europeans permeates his scholarship, posited as early as 1909 that Cypro-Minoan descended from Minoan Linear A. In his hands, Cypro-Minoan inscriptions were taken as proof of European ingenuity and Europe's pivotal role in the spread of writing from west to east (Vidal, 2014). Evans posited that a small but influential group of Minoans colonized parts of Cyprus and the Levantine coast, where they invented not only Cypro-Minoan but also the alphabet (Evans, 1909, pp. 74, 77). If the invention of writing could not be claimed by Europe, since that honor belonged to the cuneiform writing of Iraq and the hieroglyphs of Egypt, Evans wove a tale in which "European" Minoans invented the most ingenious and efficient of writing systems, the alphabet.

Today, no scholars believe that "Minoan" Linear A was the progenitor of the Phoenician alphabet. Studies show that the alphabet is no more efficient than syllabic and logographic writing systems, and scholars question the value of applying the very modern, Western concept of efficiency to ancient contexts. Nevertheless, the myth of the alphabet's efficiency persists (Baroni, 2011). The idea that Minoans created the alphabet was always a transparent attempt by Evans to disassociate the alphabet from the "oriental" Levant and transport it to the "European" Aegean. The signs of the Phoenician alphabet are clearly modeled Egyptian and hieratic signs according to the acrophonic principle, where the first letter of the word depicted by the hieroglyph becomes the sign's sound value (e.g., the first letter of the Phoenician alphabet "aleph" derives from a hieroglyphic sign depicting an ox's head, or *alef*, in Semitic languages).

After Evans, the next scholar to look at Cypro-Minoan was Menalaos Markides, the first Curator of the Cyprus Museum from 1912 to 1931. The

Greek Cypriot Markides was a pioneer of scientific archaeological methods and applied the same level-headed circumspection to Cypro-Minoan (Pilides, 2018). Even during the war years when the museum's budget was mean, Markides went to great effort to continue excavations and document the island's past. He was rewarded with the discoveries of eleven new Cypro-Minoan texts, comprised exclusively of short multisign and single-sign vessel texts. Markides published them, along with a signary, in short reports in consecutive years, 1915 and 1916. Markides's signary counted some twenty-two unique signs, thirteen of which he attributed to Aegean origins and the rest not (Markides, 1916).

Subsequent European scholars returned to Evans's Aegeo-centric interpretation of the script. Swedish excavations in the 1920s added to the list of Cypro-Minoan texts, again mostly in the form of short and single-sign vessel texts. These were published along with a signary by the Swedish archaeologist Axel Persson, discussed in Section 2, who took an unabashedly Eurocentric approach to the script, so sure the inscriptions were written in Greek that he attempted a decipherment to that effect. The British colonial officer and scholar Stanley Casson was much more measured than Persson in his inventory of signs and interpretation of the script but did little to advance the study of Cypro-Minoan beyond the Evans paradigm. Of the four scholars responsible for the early studies of Cypro-Minoan, only Markides, the Greek Cypriot, questioned the wholesale European origins of the script.

Perhaps the most innovative pre-War approach to Cypro-Minoan was taken by the American archaeologist and World War II spy John Franklin Daniel, mentioned in Section 2. Daniel created a classification system that sorted texts by their material features, the method in which they were inscribed (incised after firing vs. impressed before firing), and the origins of their writing medium (imported vs. exported). Like Markides, he theorized that some classes of Cypro-Minoan inscriptions were not Aegean inventions but Cypriot ones.

3.2 One Cypro-Minoan or Three?

Debates over script and ethnicity in the study of Cypro-Minoan took a strange turn in the second half of the 20th century. The two archaeologists leading separate digs at Enkomi, the Greek Cypriot Porphyrios Dikaios and the French aristocrat Claude F. A. Schaeffer, engaged in an acrimonious battle over the date when Achaean (i.e., Greek) Trojan war heroes colonized Cyprus per Homer (their feud was so bitter that a whole book has been written about it, Papasavvas, 2023). Schaeffer also posited the colonization of the island by "Semites." Epigraphists, for their part, mined the paleography of Cypro-Minoan inscriptions for signs of the ethnic identity of their writers. Lines rendered in

A   B   C

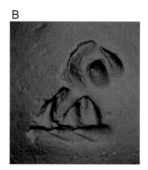

Figure 10 3D models of Cypro-Minoan signs. A. CM 102 incised into ivory (##162 KITI Iins 002); B. CM 041 impressed into wet clay (##018 ENKO Abou 016); C. CM 102 incised into hard clay (##128 KATY Avas 002).

Courtesy of Polig and Donnelly, 2022.

a supposedly "linear" or "drawn" manner reminiscent of Linear A and B were attributed to ethnically "Aegean" writers, while lines rendered in a supposedly more "cuneiformized" or "impressed" technique to ethnically "Semitic" writers (see Figure 10). Much Cypro-Minoan scholarship from this period flattens the ingenuity and paleographical diversity of Cypro-Minoan in favor of assigning ethnic labels.

3.2.1 "Achaean" Tablets?

Some of the fiercest debates over the ethnic identity of Cypro-Minoan writers focused on the seven clay tablets, three from Enkomi and four from Ugarit, discovered in quick succession in the 1950s (Ferrara argues there are four clay tablets from Enkomi, Ferrara, 2012, pp. 192–195). The Enkomi tablets were, in the hands of Dikaios, evidence of the Greek colonization of; in the hands of Schaeffer, evidence of Semitic colonizers. That two scholars could arrive at diametrically opposed conclusions looking at the same artifacts, both conclusions based in colonialist fantasies, speaks more about the political climate in which the discovery of the tablets took place than the features of the tablets.

Porphyrios Dikaios was the Curator of the Cyprus Museum (1932–1960) and the first Director of the Department of Antiquities, Cyprus after independence (1960–1963). Dapper and cosmopolitan, the Nicosia-born Dikaios was selected by the colonial government, like Markides before him, to receive archaeological training abroad. Like Markides, Dikaios returned to the island and implemented a level of scientific rigor in his excavations that superseded most of his contemporaries working on Cyprus and elsewhere. Dikaios was assigned by the

Department of Antiquities, Cyprus, to excavate at Enkomi concurrently with French Expedition excavations at Enkomi led by Schaeffer as a stopgap against what were considered the latter's destructive excavation methods (Papasavvas, 2023, p. 41).

Dikaios excavated two of the site's three clay tablets (##207 and ##208) in consecutive years, 1952 and 1953, finding them in contexts he dated roughly to the 12th century just after the "collapse." The dating coincided well with his theory that the island was colonized by Achaean Greek refugees in the aftermath of the destruction of the Mycenaean palaces. For Dikaios, the "Achaean" authorship of the two tablets was never in question. Given the opportunity to publish the tablets, as is customary for the lead excavator, he selected Aegean scripts specialists John L. Myres, nicknamed "Blackbeard" for his World War I naval espionage, and Michael Ventris, the decipherer of the Linear B script, to collaborate with him (Dikaios, 1953, 1956). Although Dikaios was known for his impartial and apolitical public persona, it is hard not to see his theory of Achaean colonizers and his choice to call them by the Homeric term "Achaean" as an attempt, con-scious or not, to ground modern Cypriot identity in a Greekness dating back to the imagined age of Homeric heroes.

Claude Schaeffer, the lead excavator of the French Expedition at Enkomi and at Ugarit, disagreed vociferously with Dikaios's dating and interpretation of the Enkomi tablets. Schaeffer's disagreements were rooted in his belief that an Achaean colonization of Cyprus had happened earlier in the 14th century and that the 12th-century "collapse" period marked the colonization of Cyprus by the Sea Peoples, whom he believed to be ethnically Semitic. An earlier 14th-century date for the Achaean invasion allowed Schaeffer to posit that Ugarit was a Mycenaean (i.e., Greek) colony, an echo of Evans's theory that the Phoenician alphabet was invented by Europeans.

Schaeffer recruited Cypro-Minoan to support his theory of successive colo-nizations. He "read" the shapes of sign on the Enkomi and Ugarit tablets as if they were clues indicative of the ethnicity of their writers. In the Ugarit tablets, he found "linear" paleography characteristic of ethnic "Mycenaeans," and in the Enkomi tablet a "cuneiform" aspect characteristic of ethnic Semites. His method of reading ethnicity into sign shapes which is a reduction to absurdity, nevertheless supplied the germ for a theory cultivated and popularized in the subsequent decades, that Cypro-Minoan represented not one single script but three subscripts representing three languages, one belonging to Cyprus (CM 1), another to the supposed immigrants to Enkomi who made the tablets (CM 2), and another to Ugarit (CM 3).

That the clay tablets became a focal point for fantasies about ethnicity and colonization in the 1950s and 1960s echoes the intensity of the anticolonial struggle of the 1950s and the tumultuous years of independence in the 1960s. Colonial fantasies were expressed in scholarship, however, in ways that were sometimes confounding or contradictory.

3.2.2 The Paleography of the Enkomi Tablets

The Enkomi tablets ("CM 2") became the focus of ethnic theories in the 1970s (Figure 11). They were interpreted as the products of a distinct ethnic group because of the perceived unity in their material features, but even this unity is, to an extent, in the eye of the beholder. The paleography across the three tablets is certainly similar, with its compressed size and simplification of sign forms, but the same paleography was described by Émilia Masson, the main scholar of Cypro-Minoan in the 1970s, as "squared and squat" but by Myres as "Minoan," that is, drawn and linear

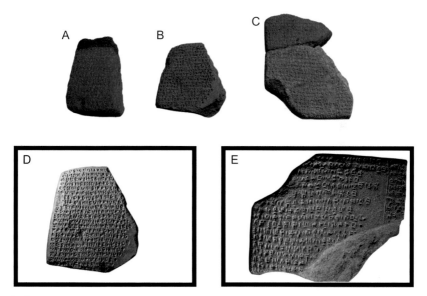

Figure 11 Enkomi tablets on display at the Cyprus Museum with close-ups. A. ##209 ENKO Atab 004; B. ##208 ENKO Atab 003; C. ##207 ENKO Atab 002. Note that ##209 is a cast that does not reflect the true color of the tablet. D. Close-up of ##208; E. close-up of ##207. Note the similarities and differences in sign shape, ductus, and ruling.

Photographs by author, courtesy of the Cyprus Museum and the Department of Antiquities, Cyprus.

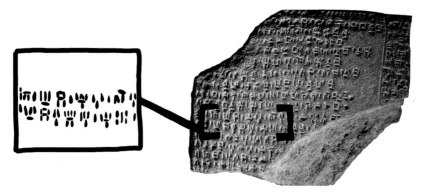

Figure 12 Close-up of ##207 showing distinctive Enkomi tablet paleography.

Photograph by author, autopsy courtesy of the Cyprus Museum and the Department of Antiquities, Cyprus.

(see Figure 12; Masson, 1974, p. 15; Dikaios, 1956). Aside from the paleography and line ruling, the tablets are different from one another in the color of their clay, tablet shape, and formatting. The perceived uniformity between the Enkomi tablets nevertheless became the basis for the claims that they were written by a distinctive ethnic group.

3.2.3 Masson's Trifold Division of the Script

Émilia Masson's trifold division of Cypro-Minoan into the CM 1, CM 2, and CM 3 subscripts is heavily influential in Aegean scripts studies and Cypriot archaeology (Table 2). Masson distinguished the subscripts by what she believed to be their distinctive paleography and sign repertoires, which she associated with the different linguistic and therefore ethnic identities of their writers: CM 1 was the script of local Cypriots, CM 2 of Hurrian (i.e., Anatolian) immigrants to Enkomi, and CM 3 of Ugaritians (Masson, 1974). In a departure from Dikaios and Schaeffer, whose debates centered on Greeks and Semites, Masson's main "ethnic" players were indigenous Cypriots and Anatolians. The influence of Greece is relegated to a bit part, relevant only to the earliest Cypro-Minoan inscriptions, and the influence of "Semites" is restricted to the inscriptions found in Ugarit.

The changing political landscape on the island in the 1970s and the simplistic worldview that equates language, script, and identity provide a context for Masson's subdivision. Writing mainly in the 1970s, Masson's theory of the Hurrian origins of the CM 2 Enkomi tablets coincides with the Turkish (Anatolian) occupation, encompassing the northern third of the island including the site of Enkomi. Although the timing might seem overly coincidental, as seen

Table 2 Émilia Masson's subscript division

Subscript	Paleographic style	Language	Ethnic group
CM 1	Linear/diverse	Cypriot/unidentified	Local Cypriot
CM 2	Squared	Hurrian	Hurrian
CM 3	"Cuneiformized"	Semitic	Ugaritian

throughout this section, it is often the case that scholarship is influenced by contemporary politics. It can be no coincidence, for instance, that this Element fixates on "collapse" during a moment of heightened global crisis. Hurrian speakers, who we met in Section 1 in relation to the Amarna Letters and the Kingdom of Mitanni, were major players in the Late Bronze Age. In that sense, her focus on Hurrians was not out of place. According to Masson's theory, Hurrian-speakers were a cohesive ethnic group who, displaced from their homeland in Mitanni by invading Hittites, relocated to Enkomi where they adapted the Cypro-Minoan script to write their language (see Figure 13). Her theory is not corroborated, however, by other archaeological evidence. For Masson, the inscriptions were proof enough: A script's paleography and the language it recorded revealed the ethnicity of its writers.

Masson's subdivision ultimately suffers from the faulty assumption that ethnic difference can be reduced to linguistic difference and that linguistic difference is expressed in script choice. One of the takeaways from this Element, I hope, is the lesson that script and language are not the same. Masson's subdivision is based on both real and perceived differences among Cypro-Minoan inscriptions but flattens those exciting differences in favor of the old colonial and archaeological obsession with ethnicity.

3.3 The Era of the Corpus and Beyond (2007–Today)

Up until 2007, there was no up-to-date list of Cypro-Minoan inscriptions, with the result that the field was extremely hard to access for beginners, and even seasoned scholars had trouble writing synopses of the script and its uses. Émilia Masson's career coincided with a flood of new Cypro-Minoan texts in the 1960s and 1970s and, perhaps to keep up with the pace of discovery, her publications were piecemeal, short articles and excavation reports. In some ways, her work anticipates the materialist focus of the present Element and its concern with document forms. For instance, Masson's longest Cypro-Minoan publication is a study only of clay balls, albeit only the ones excavated by Schaeffer (Masson, 1971). In other ways, her work is a product of its time, obsessed with paleography as an expression of ethnic origins at the expense of the other material

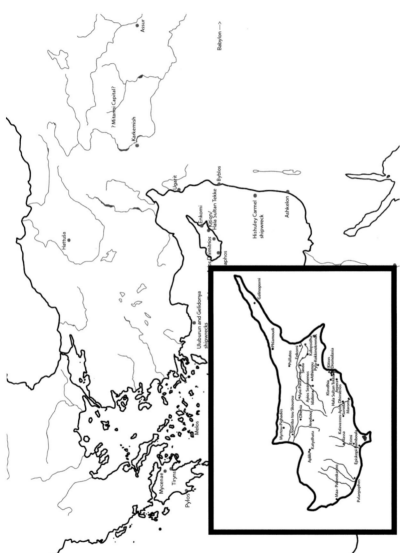

Figure 13 Map of Cyprus in context, indicating sites on Cyprus with Cypro-Minoan inscriptions.

features of the inscriptions. In fact, she rarely described the material features of the objects she studied. The early 2000s therefore found the field of Cypro-Minoan studies in need of critical reexamination.

The field of Cypriot archaeology, and archaeology more widely, has moved away from its obsession with ethnic origins and the simplistic attribution of distinctive material cultures to colonizing ethnic groups (sometimes called the "pots = people" approach to archaeology). Scholarship has begun to focus on Cyprus as Cyprus, without overemphasizing the role of colonizers or colonization in shaping the island's history. In the contemporary social sphere, Cypriot identities based on a shared pan-island identity have emerged. The study of Cypro-Minoan has likewise been influenced by more Cypro-centric approaches to the island's history and identity, with the result that interregionality is sometimes overlooked.

The past two decades in Cypro-Minoan studies changed the field in two significant ways. First, two comprehensive lists of Cypro-Minoan texts (called a corpus, pl. corpora) were finally published (Olivier, 2007; Ferrara, 2013). Interested scholars from any field could now find Cypro-Minoan inscriptions all in one place. Second, both corpora broke with the tradition of including single-sign texts in their lists of inscriptions. Alongside the corpora came new sociohistorical and diachronic approaches to the study of writing on Cyprus, concerned with the social roles of the island's writers and writing Cyprus. These studies still sometimes included the single-sign texts in their analysis but more often focus on the multisign texts. Currently, the field stands at an impasse as it seeks to understand the role of single-sign texts in the transmission of Cypro-Minoan.

3.3.1 HoChyMin

It was not until 2007 with the publication of Jean-Pierre Olivier's *Édition holistique des textes chypro-minoens*, known by its acronym *HoChyMin*, that an official corpus of Cypro-Minoan inscriptions was published. The Belgian scholar had a long history of publishing the corpora of undeciphered scripts. In partnership with Louis Godart, he had published the corpus of Linear A, which goes by the delightful acronym *GORILA*, and that of the Cretan hieroglyphic script, the modish *CHIC*. *HoChyMin* was a departure from the other corpora, not only in its head-scratching acronym but also in being an *édition holistique* or "holistic edition."

Traditionally, Aegean script corpora are compiled by a person or team who organizes and publishes (or republishes) as much information as possible about all recorded inscriptions in a given script. A corpus either is the first publication of new inscriptions from the site or, in the case of subsequent editions, republishes older inscriptions and adds new ones. The case of Cypro-Minoan was different in that inscriptions had already been published, just not assembled, hence "holistic edition." Olivier understood his remit to be the assembly of a "un patchwork composé avec les membra disjecta" ("a patchwork composed of dismembered parts"), a phrase I quote in the original French for its mélange of French, English, and Latin, a great example of how language identification based on short snippets of text can be misleading (Olivier, 2007, p. 16).

　　Olivier did not find his job of assembling the Cypro-Minoan patchwork easy. The large number of sites (20+) where Cypro-Minoan writing has been found, the over 600-year timespan in which Cypro-Minoan was in use, and the large number of short or damaged texts whose status as writing is ambiguous posed considerable problems. He suspected even at the time of publication that he had omitted or missed inscriptions due to time and age constraints (Olivier, 2007, p. 16). The unwieldiness of the corpus required him to make difficult choices about which texts to include and exclude. Ultimately, he chose to exclude single-sign texts from the corpus even if he believed many to be writing. There were simply too many, from too many different sites (*membra disjecta*) to assemble within a reasonable time frame. Excluding them had the benefit of providing uniformity to what was included, namely texts with two or more contiguous script signs written on the same plane. As Olivier suspected, it is now clear that his corpus is missing inscriptions, around eighty, most on vessels, published in obscure publications or in short reports.

　　HoChyMin benefited Cypro-Minoan studies greatly in that it provided scholars with the first synoptic view of the script since the flood of new inscriptions discovered in the 1950–1970s. Olivier organized the inscriptions according to an ingenious system that encodes an inscription's writing medium and findspot in its corpus number. For instance, the eighth recovered vessel inscription from Kition was given the corpus number ##137 KITI Avas 008 (see Figure 14). Less helpfully, inscriptions were published usually without accompanying images of the objects they appear on. Olivier also adhered to Masson's subscript division despite his reservations concerning its utility (*HoChyMin*, p. 16) and even added a new subscript designation, CM 0, for the earliest "intermediate" Enkomi tablet ##001 ENKO Atab 001, discussed in Section 1.

3.3.2 CM II

A focus on materiality is evident in the second corpus of Cypro-Minoan inscriptions, *CM II*, published shortly on the heels of *HoChyMin* in 2013 by the Italian scholar Silvia Ferrara. Following the suggestion of American

##137 KITI Avas 008

= unique corpus number   KITI = site abbreviation   A = abbreviation of   vas = object type   008 = 8th object of the same type and
material (in French)   (in French)   material from the same site

Figure 14 Olivier's inscription numbering system. Also adopted by Ferrara in
CM II (2013).

Drawing by author based on autopsy, courtesy of the Cyprus Museum and the
Department of Antiquities, Cyprus.

scholars Nicolle Hirschfeld and Joanna Smith, Ferrara's catalogue of inscriptions foregrounds archaeological context over paleography and, for the first time, provides photographs of the objects on which inscriptions appear as opposed to only its text (Smith and Hirschfeld, 1999). Thanks to this decision, it is possible for scholars to observe the material aspects of each inscription without having to travel to museum storerooms. In addition to the catalogue of inscriptions, she published a compendium "Analysis" volume, *CM I*, where in 2012 she analyzed the materiality of Cypro-Minoan inscriptions and contextualized Cypro-Minoan writing practices within the island and outside of it.

Ferrara's *CM II* is also innovative for doing away with Masson's subdivision, a decision which she explains in *CM I*. In other ways, however, it is overly faithful to *HoChyMin* and replicates many of its omissions and mistakes. While *CM II* adds over thirty new inscriptions, around fifty inscriptions remain unpublished or uncollected. Single-sign texts were again excluded, but on different grounds. For Ferrara, it is impossible to judge whether a specific single-sign text represents a writing or marking system.

3.4 Materiality and Single-Sign Texts

The question of whether to count single-sign texts as writing had first been dealt with in earnest by John Franklin Daniel, who developed a method for distinguishing script from nonscript signs in the single-sign texts. Having just excavated eighty new Cypro-Minoan texts, most single-sign vessel texts, he sought to create an accurate signary that maximized the number of identifiable script signs but also excluded nonscript signs (See Section 2.2.2; Daniel, 1941). He had correctly intuited that not all signs recorded in the single-sign texts were script signs. Since Daniel's World War II days, the significance of the single-sign texts has changed. Shapes of script signs drawn from single-sign texts are no longer considered in the construction of signaries; instead, single-sign texts bear on questions about the spread of literacy and writing on Cyprus. The single-sign texts are more numerous than multisign texts (1,500+ compared to c. 300), with the implication that Cypro-Minoan writing would have been more common and visible to a wider audience than the more limited multisign corpus alone suggests.

Assessed in terms of materiality, the single-sign texts belong to the same document form as the multisign texts. For Nicolle Hirschfeld, who laid the foundations for the study of single-sign texts on vessels (referred to as "potmarks" in Cypro-Minoan studies), separating out the multisign vessel texts from the single-sign vessel texts was never a consideration: They follow the same patterns of materiality, vessel selection, text placement, and construction and come from the same types of archaeological contexts (see Figure 15; Hirschfeld 1999, 2002). Joanna Smith likewise included single-sign texts in her study of writing practices at the site of Kourion, seeing no separation in the archaeological contexts and inscription habits of multisign and single-sign texts (Smith, 2012).

Both text types are sometimes treated as evidence of literacy. Philippa Steele, who has written a lovely and accessible history of writing on Cyprus (Steele, 2019), treats single-sign vessel texts as evidence of writing and literacy, noting that any distinction between them "in terms of ... function and context ... is entirely a false one" (Steele, 2017, p. 157). The institutional contexts of their writers and readership/viewership are indistinguishable. Susan Sherratt, an archaeologist with a keen interest in Cyprus and the "postcollapse" economy of the eastern Mediterranean, takes a slightly different approach, interpreting the single-sign vessel texts as evidence for what she calls "literacy-awareness," the ability to recognize writing as writing without necessarily being able to identify, translate, or reproduce every phoneme in a script (Sherratt, 2003, p. 226).

A single document form comprising texts that are certainly writing (multisign texts), certainly not writing (single-sign texts with nonscript signs), and ambiguous (single-sign texts with script signs) complicates our definitions of writing and literacy. A strict definition of writing would regard single-sign texts

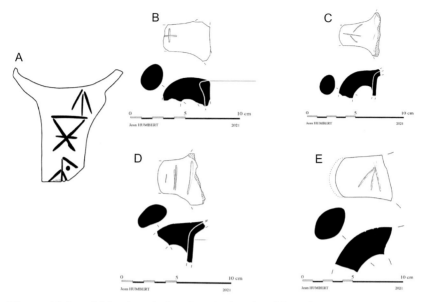

Figure 15 A multisign inscription from Enkomi and four single-sign texts from Kition. A. Multisign inscription from Enkomi missing from *HoChyMin* and *CM II*, CM 17.46. B. Text with ambiguous script/nonscript sign, KB 18–603; C. Text with sign that used to be regarded as a script sign but no longer is, K18-523; D. Text with nonscript sign K18-120; E. Text with likely script sign, K18-249. All drawings by Jean Humbert.

Drawing of CM 17.46 by author based on autopsy, courtesy of the Cyprus Museum and the Department of Antiquities, Cyprus.

Drawings of the Kition handles by Jean Humbert. © Mission archéologique de Kition, Jean Humbert.

as writing only if they represent a phoneme, that is, a spoken language sound (either a monosyllabic word or an abbreviation of a longer word). Literacy would constitute the ability to recognize which phoneme is represented by the script sign and to correctly interpret it. It is with this definition in mind that Ferrara dismisses the single-sign texts from her corpus. She believes it is impossible to assess how a single script sign written on an object thousands of years ago would have been read (Ferrara 2013, p. 4). Hirschfeld, Smith, Steele, and Sherratt entertain a wider definition of literacy and see continuity between the nonscript and multisign vessel texts.

When building a picture of the Cypro-Minoan script and its writers, including single-sign texts in the frame, "it seems hard to escape the conclusion that" some form of literacy "was probably quite widespread on Cyprus at the close of the late Bronze Age" (Sherratt, 2003, p. 226). The number and types of texts, in addition to the contexts in which writing was visible, expand to include anchors, weights, ingots, architectural blocks, copper tools, and more. Many of these are objects associated with mercantile activity, especially overseas trade, and would have been handled by individuals with varying degrees of intimacy with the script (more on this in Section 4). The writers, handlers, and readers of mercantile document forms probably had different levels of "literacy." Strictly defined as the ability to recognize and correctly interpret a phoneme, only individuals trained or self-trained in the Cypro-Minoan script could be said to be literate. Others may have come to recognize patterns in the shapes and distributions of signs they saw or handled regularly and to deduce their meanings. Perhaps they were even explicitly told how to interpret the meaning of the texts, if not how to read them as phonemes.

What counts as literacy in this scenario is contingent on one's perspective. Sir Arthur Evans wanted to see single-sign texts on Bronze Age vessels as writing because his worldview required triumphal, European genius to play a feature role in the history of writing. Daniel incorporated single-sign texts in the construction of his signary because he only had limited data to work with, while Olivier excluded them because he had too much data. Today, as scholarship fights (we hope!) to shed its colonial perspectives, materialist approaches to the script highlight the connections between multisign and single-sign texts (even the ones that do not record script signs) and the social circumstances in which they were produced and seen, if not read.

4 Mercantile Writers

4.1 Mercantile Texts

The most unique aspect of Cypro-Minoan vis à vis its neighbors and for the history of Late Bronze Age Mediterranean writing generally is the significant proportion of texts on objects implicated in overseas trade. Cypro-Minoan texts on mercantile objects remain understudied. In the past decade alone, new Cypro-Minoan texts have been identified at Tiryns, Greece, in the Cyclades, in shipwrecks off the coast of Anatolia and the Levant, and in the southern Levant Philistine site of Ashkelon. The texts on mercantile objects are short and therefore uninformative for decipherment but reveal plenty about the role of writing in trade (see Table 3). The most common mercantile texts are on vessels (1,500+), on ingots of various metals (c. 100 texts), and on copper tools (c. 20 texts). The types of vessels bearing texts, the ingots, and the copper tools, which were used for scrap, are objects associated with Cypriot trade. The involvement of Cyprus in the trade of these objects is assured by the distribution of the objects within and outside of Cyprus, the mix of imported and exported objects

Table 3 Mercantile document forms

Copper tools		
	Enkomi	6 (1 unpublished BM 1896,0401.1467)
	Hishuley Carmel	1 (Valério and Davis, 2017, fig. 7)
	Gelidonya	1 (Blackwell et al. forthcoming cat. no. 9)
	Pyla-*Kokkinokremos*	1
Tin ingots		
	Hishuley Carmel	4 (Galili, 2013)
Vessel inscriptions		
	Arpera	1
	Athienou	2
	Dhenia	1
	Enkomi	24 (10 not recorded in the corpora)
	Hala Sultan Tekke	1
	Idalion	3
	Kalavasos-*Ayios Dhimitrios*	2
	Kalopsidha	1
	Katydhata	3
	Kition	31
	Klavdia-*Tremithos*	1
	Kourion	13 (6 not recorded in the corpora)
	Maa-*Palaeokastro*	4
	Maroni-*Vournes*	4
	Myrtou-*Pighades*	2
	Sanidha	1
	Tiryns	2
	Toumba tou Skourou	2
	Ugarit	3
	Total:	**114**
Outliers		
Clay cylinders		
	Enkomi	1
	Kalavasos-*Ayios Dhimitrios*	5

Table 3 (cont.)

Tablets		
	Enkomi	3 (or 4, see Ferrara 2012, p. 193)
	Pyla-*Kokkinokremos*	2 (Polig, 2022)
	Ras Shamra	4
	Total:	**15**

bearing texts, and the fact that most texts on mercantile objects were made after firing. The most reasonable inference is that the texts were made by Cyprus-based traders who handled the objects en route from or to their destination (Hirschfeld, 2004; Yasur-Landau, 2017). The texts likely refer to the traders themselves and not to the traded objects, since the same or similar texts appear on different types of traded objects.

Cypro-Minoan is distinctive for its substantial number of texts on mercantile objects. "Mercantile objects" include not only imports and exports but also goods handled by Cypriot merchants acting as middlemen. A small portion of mercantile texts with simple lines and crosses may record commercial information, such as numerals, but by and large the texts do not contain commercial information pertaining to the content of vessels or the movements of goods. It is theorized that the texts refer to the individual trader or group of traders (Hirschfeld, 2004). Tin ingots recovered from shipwrecks support the idea that the texts refer to individuals and groups of traders working as middlemen because tin was not produced on Cyprus (Galili et al., 2013). Tin was likely imported into the Mediterranean, perhaps from far as afield as Cornwall in Britain, or Afghanistan, or closer to home from the Anatolian interior (Berger et al., 2019). Cypro-Minoan texts on tin ingots recovered from the eastern Mediterranean seabed could only have been incised by merchant middlemen.

The practice of regularly writing on mercantile objects is unique to Cyprus in the Late Bronze Age. Linear B's use is restricted almost exclusively to purpose-made administrative documents, in the form of clay tablets and labels. The tablets also rarely mention trade, concerned instead with the internal administration and distribution of goods, enslaved people, and administrative agents. Some goods and enslaved people are marked as "foreign" and would have necessarily been imported into the Mycenaean sphere, but the texts never refer to the mechanics of trade or to "traders" and never record trade transactions (Nikoloudis, 2010). Cuneiform texts from palatial contexts are likewise purpose-made administrative documents, clay tablets and seals. Cuneiform texts testify to both royal and trade activities, but the texts tend not to appear on mercantile objects themselves. The frequency of mercantile writing on Cyprus, as compared to its neighbors, could reflect a difference in attitudes toward who was allowed to see and practice writing. Mercantile objects would necessarily have been seen and handled by literate and nonliterate individuals, unlike tablets and seals, access to which could have been easily restricted to their writers and readers working directly with them.

On Cyprus, not only were some traders literate, but they advertised their ability by marking objects that would travel widely both within and outside of Cyprus. For instance, vessel handle document form inscriptions were incised after firing deeply and clearly on vessel handles, visible to anyone in the vessel's immediate vicinity. Depending on when the vessel was inscribed during its mercantile journey, its various handlers would not only have seen the inscription but touched it while grabbing the vessel and moving it from place to place. Some vessel handle texts intentionally confront their audience with writing. A wonderful example is a single-sign text painted onto the inside surface of a shallow decorated Mycenaean cup originating in Greece but found in a tomb at Enkomi (see Figure 16). The cup is of a type used in communal rituals related to wine consumption. As someone drank dark wine from it, they would find themselves, in their final draughts, face to face with Cypro-Minoan sign CM 027, painted in thick, clear lines.

The idea that signs on mercantile objects refer to traders or groups of traders originates in part from the fact that the same signs appear again and again across the different types of mercantile objects. Take CM 027, the sign painted on the interior of the Mycenaean cup just mentioned. The same sign occurs incised on different types of vessels, stamped prominently into the surface of a copper ingot, incised into the surface of a copper tool found in the Gelidonya shipwreck (see Figure 16), and incised clearly into the face of an anchor reused as building material at Hala Sultan Tekke. The diversity of objects bearing the same sign highlights this sign's association with the movement of goods, not a specific type of material. Nor is the sign apparently linked to place. Mercantile objects bearing CM 027 are widespread, found in the Aegean, the eastern Mediterranean, and throughout Cyprus. It is therefore possible but unlikely the sign refers to either a production or destination site. Instead, the sign may be an abbreviation of the first letter of a word or name referring to an individual trader or, more likely, a group of traders.

CM 027 would not be unusual in being an abbreviation. Many of the texts on mercantile objects probably contain abbreviations (Donnelly, 2022a). The structure of texts on mercantile objects is consistent across different types of objects, an indication that texts to belong to the same "family" texts, which were produced by traders. Most texts on mercantile inscriptions are two-sign

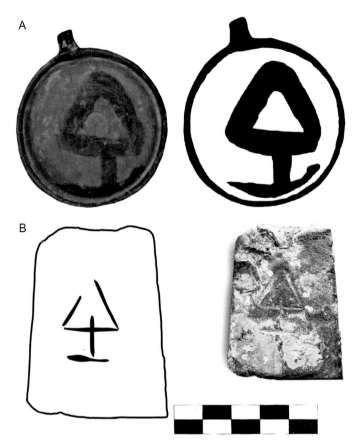

Figure 16 Two single-sign mercantile texts with CM 027. A. CM 027 painted
on the interior of a Mycenaean cup from Enkomi.

Photograph and drawing by author, courtesy of the Cyprus Museum and the Department
of Antiquities, Cyprus.

B. CM 027 incised into a copper tool from the Cape Gelidonya shipwreck, B111.

Photograph by John Littlefield, courtesy of the Institute of Nautical Archaeology.

inscriptions, 1 + 1 inscriptions with the structure "sign word-divider sign," or
single-sign texts, including ones with script and nonscript signs (Karageorghis
and Masson, 1971). The 1 + 1 inscriptions are almost certainly abbreviations,
given the presence of the word divider. What is perhaps unexpected is that two-
sign texts appear to be interchangeable with 1 + 1 inscriptions, as they certainly
are in the case of the inscribed miniature ingots. The four ingots contain the
same two-sign sequence, sometimes with a word divider and sometimes without. The two-sign sequence clearly abbreviates the five-sign sequence on ingot
##175 Mlin 002 in some form (see Figure 17). Though the precise function of

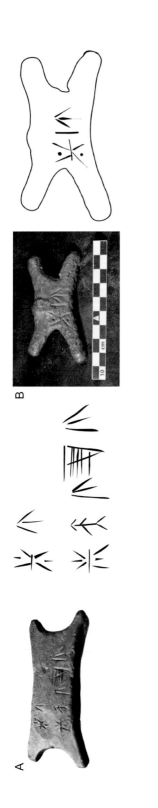

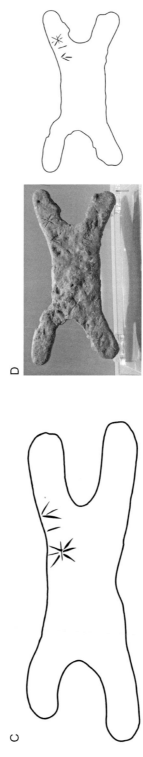

Figure 17 Four miniature ingots. A. ##175 ENKO Mlin 002; B. ##174 ENKO Mlin 001; C. ##176 ENKO Mlin 003; D. ADD##260 CYPR Mlin 001.

Photographs and drawings of ingots ##174–176 by author, courtesy of the Cyprus Museum and the Department of Antiquities, Cyprus. Photograph of ADD##260 by Anna Spyrou, permission courtesy of the Leventis Municipal Museum of Nicosia.

miniature ingots remains a matter of debate (were they votive objects? proto-types advertising "normal"-sized copper ingots?), their form represents oxhide ingots, one of Cyprus's main goods for export in the Late Bronze Age (for different interpretations, see Ferrara and Bell, 2016; Giumlia-Mair et al., 2011; Meneghetti, 2022). The ingots provide a good case study for abbreviations because they show a two-sign inscription used interchangeably with a 1 + 1 inscription on two different ingots. The principle observed on the miniature ingots, of two-sign inscriptions being used interchangeably with 1 + 1 inscriptions, is likely applicable to the whole of mercantile texts.

Many single-sign texts, too, can be convincingly shown to be word abbreviations. Take, for instance, three texts incised on Mycenaean vessels found in the same tomb at Kition, ##131 KITI Avas 002, T.9/51, and T.9/36. Vessel ##131 has a two-sign text painted on the lower part of a vessel jug, CM 004–026. The other two have the same single-sign text, CM 026, incised onto their handles, the second sign in the sequence on ##131. Since the texts were found together, it is reasonable to infer that each is an abbreviation referring to the same thing (whatever it may be). This same phenomenon is apparent in the aforementioned collection of tin ingots: Four tin ingots share the same two signs, CM 019 and 082, and one ingot with a single sign bears CM 019. Because they were found together, it is almost certain that the single-sign text and multisign texts have the same referent. The interpretation of single-sign texts, however, is rarely as clear-cut as the examples just discussed. At least some of the single-sign texts with script signs are abbreviations, but others inhabit a space somewhere between writing and nonphonetic marking.

The lines distinguishing writing from marking on mercantile objects are extremely blurry. Texts with both script and nonscript signs belong to the same document form. Texts on copper tools illustrate this ambiguity well. Copper tools form an interesting body of mercantile texts because their mercantile associations are not readily apparent. Their associations with trade arise from a mix of archaeological and textual evidence. Over 800 copper tools were found in the Gelidonya shipwreck, believed to be the cargo of a traveling copper merchant who would have sold the metal as scrap for remelting (Hirschfeld, 2019). Cuneiform texts from Ugarit also register copper tools as ship's cargoes and even as forms of payment in some cases (Routledge and McGeough, 2009). There are twenty-one texts on copper tools, ten multisign inscriptions and eleven single-sign texts belonging to the same document form. Among the single-sign texts, some contain script signs that are common on other mercantile objects, such as the aforementioned copper tool from the Gelidonya shipwreck with CM 027 incised prominently on its surface (Figure 16). Other tools with single-sign texts contain nonscript signs also observed on other mercantile objects. Given all that, is the CM 027 on the tool writing or not? It is hard to say.

It is likely that script and nonscript signs on the same document form are analogous in function, denoting an individual or group of traders. The continuity between the signs used as abbreviations in the two-sign and single-sign texts on the same document form would indicate that single-sign texts belong to the writing system. But when the single-sign texts do not contain script signs, they are clearly not writing. The mercantile texts seem to be a hodgepodge, mixing script and nonscript signs to the same end. They do not fall easily into one category or the other. In Section 5, when we look at nonmercantile or insular texts, we will see much less continuity between script and nonscript signs, but they share the same heavy use of abbreviations.

4.2 Mercantile Writers

The merchants who wrote Cypro-Minoan come alive to us through their texts. Mercantile institutions are largely invisible in the archaeological record. Because the texts on mercantile objects seem to refer to the merchant handlers themselves, the mercantile texts become invaluable for reconstructing the number and organization of overseas merchants. Contemporary texts from Ugarit also help with the reconstruction. Overall, the image that emerges is of many small groups of merchants conducting overseas trade (McGeough, 2015). Trade organizations are seemingly not tightly bound to administrative institutions on Cyprus, raising interesting questions about how the script was transmitted among and between traders. The backdrop of economic upheaval adds complexity to the story. Were the literate traders on Cyprus adapting writing in new ways during the collapse period, or were their activities somehow under the radar, only coming to the fore when neighboring polities collapsed?

4.2.1 The Precollapse Decades: Cypro-Minoan Writers at Ugarit

Most mercantile texts date to the LCIIC and LCIIIA periods on both sides of the "Bronze Age collapse." It is fascinating to wonder whether the traders active in the LCIIC could feel the shifting tides in their overseas networks, or if the traders at Ugarit could sense their city's impending destruction. Testimonials in letters from Ugarit speak to a level of anxiety, decreased grain supply, hunger in outlying regions, and attacks from the "people of the sea." Yet other documents record the activities of elite merchants traveling and conducting business unencumbered. One of these merchants, a man named Yabninu, who was also a high administrator (*šatammu rabu*) in the royal bureaucracy of Ugarit, had such close ties to Cyprus that both mercantile and nonmercantile Cypro-Minoan document forms were found in his home (for a great social history of writing at Ugarit, which puts Yabninu in context, see Boyes, 2021). The ease of mobility implied by Yabninu's cache of Cypro-Minoan texts speaks to traders' continued engagement in overseas exchange on the precipice of collapse and reveals the closeness of the networks established by traders.

Yabninu was a senior official in the kingdom of Ugarit who also worked as a merchant and (perhaps) envoy at the end of the 13th century. The more elite the merchant at Ugarit, the freer he was to conduct personal trade in addition to official, royal business (McGeough, 2015). Yabninu's house contained ample evidence for close personal and official relationships between himself and people outside of Ugarit. The house contains fine imports from throughout the eastern Mediterranean, including Cyprus, and just under 100 tablets recording the administration of foreign residents at Ugarit and evincing close mercantile ties with Cyprus, Phoenicia, Palestine, and Egypt. Among the tablets, most written in syllabic cuneiform, were two written in Cypro-Minoan. More indicative of close ties to Cyprus than the tablets, perhaps, are the array of mercantile texts scattered throughout the house, single-sign and multisign texts on a mix of local and imported vessels (see Figure 18). Not only do we know through

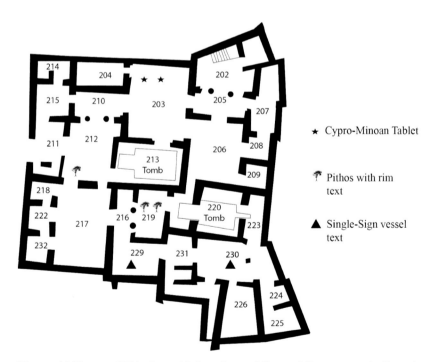

Figure 18 House of Yabninu with locations of Cypro-Minoan texts indicated. Drawn by author based on Boyes, 2021.

cuneiform texts that Yabninu traded with Cyprus and knew Cypriot merchants, but his house contained a set of vessel texts that would have been right at home on Cyprus.

Indications that traders from Ugarit, as opposed to persons from another walk of life, were likely involved in the transmission of Cypro-Minoan to Ugarit come from the large numbers of single-sign vessel texts on local and imported vessels found throughout the city and its port, Minet el-Beida (Hirschfeld, 2004). Of less clear significance are the findspots of the Cypro-Minoan inscriptions, most of which were found in the homes of traders, since most inscriptions of any kind at Ugarit come from the homes of elite traders. The vessel texts on imported and local vessels indicate the involvement of traders in the production of Cypro-Minoan texts at Ugarit, not simply the importation of Cypro-Minoan texts from Cyprus.

The local adaptation of Cypro-Minoan writing at Ugarit is further evident in the creative adaptation of Cypro-Minoan document forms and the invention of new ones. For instance, four of the twelve Cypro-Minoan texts from Ugarit are tablets, "reflect[ing] experimental use" (Steele, 2019, p. 206). The tablets are not only different in document form from the Cypro-Minoan tablets from Enkomi, but they are also different from one another, each its own unique creation, displaying different formatting, punctuation, and techniques and styles of writing. The creativity on display in the Cypro-Minoan texts from Ugarit is reminiscent of the creativity displayed by writers from Ugarit more generally, who invented their own form of alphabetic cuneiform script called "Ugaritic." Experimentation bridges Cypro-Minoan and alphabetic cuneiform writing at Ugarit, making it hard to say who writers of Cypro-Minoan were. Were they merchant writers of Cypro-Minoan who set up shop at Ugarit, where they were free to reimagine their script? Merchant writers of Ugaritic, excited to learn a new script and experiment with it as they had done with their own? Our evidence is too meager to provide answers, but it raises questions about how writers at Ugarit perceived the relationship between script and identity.

We do not know if, or to what extent, script was seen as an expression of ethnic, political, or national identity in the Late Bronze Age Mediterranean, since we do not know how ethnicity or nationality were constructed or expressed. The choice to use Cypro-Minoan at Ugarit could reflect an expression of mercantile identity, not an ethnic or national one. In experimenting with the Cypro-Minoan script at Ugarit, merchants may have been asserting their identity as traders, and their identity as traders might have superseded or otherwise competed with other modes of identity like ethnicity.

4.2.2 Mercantile Institutions

How representative Yabninu was of his Cypriot counterparts in terms of mobility and a connection to "state-sponsored" interests is difficult to reconstruct. Cypro-Minoan mercantile texts contain some 80+ unique signs that may refer to an equal number of merchants or mercantile organizations (Hirschfeld, 2002). Are the 80+ signs evidence for 80 individuals as mobile and interconnected as Yabninu was? If so, on whose behalf were they working? Analogies from Ugarit are useful to a limited extent. Mercantile activity at Ugarit was driven by a mix of private and royal interests, with more autonomy to conduct personal trade given to higher-ranked persons (Routledge and McGeough, 2009). Exactly how many individuals at a given time were engaged in trade activities or how they were organized is only hinted at in the literary record. Texts from Ugarit refer to *aširuma*, a word whose translation is debated but which seems to refer to classes or groups of people, perhaps strongly associated with trade activity, under a leader (Monroe, 2009, pp. 123–125). Imagining Cypriot traders divided into corporate bodies of traders each led by a "head" is appealing. It would certainly make sense of the large but fixed groups of signs that appear on mercantile texts over the hundred-year plus period spanning the LCIIC into the LCIIIA. How such groups would obtain access to goods and on whose behalf remains to be understood, given how little is understood about the economic and political organization of Late Bronze Age Cyprus.

Traders organized into groups, conducting trade at least partially on their own behalves and with counterparts similarly arranged overseas, would have been able to transmit knowledge of writing intergenerationally and between different groups. Writing could have been taught "on the job," so to speak. A learner could have observed how to format texts properly through a mix of direct instruction and incidentally, as traders wrote on objects that entered into wide circulation. Close relationships between traders from different communities, as testified to at the house of Yabninu, would have occasioned the exchange of script knowledge, at least sporadically.

4.2.3 The Evidence from the Sea

The evidence from the sea indicates that the Cypro-Minoan script would have been visible to and used by sailors. The two most famous shipwrecks from the Bronze Age Aegean, Uluburun and Gelidonya, carry different document forms. Arrested midvoyage carrying a cargo crammed with prestige goods and raw materials of royal caliber, the mid 14th-century Uluburun wreck contained over thirty single-sign vessel texts on its transport amphorae, local Cypriot jugs, and other vessels (Pulak and Matheny, 2021). In contrast, the late 13th-century Gelidonya wreck, carrying a more quotidian cargo perhaps belonging to a traveling tinsmith, has fewer single-sign vessel texts but an intriguing group of ten copper tools, several already cut for scrap, bearing single-sign texts and a two-sign inscription (see Figure 19). The over 1,000 kilograms of total copper on the ship is believed to represent scrap metal intended for sale or remelting in port. Sailors may not have been aware of the marks and writing on their goods. Some of the texts, however, were centered on tools that had already been cut for scrap, making it likely that traders were responsible for incising signs onto the tool after they had been cut.

Clear evidence that traders wrote Cypro-Minoan signs on traded metals is seen in the ingots made from non-Cypriot metals, which have been recovered from ships sunk either en route or in harbor off the coast of modern-day Israel. The cargo of the Hishuley Carmel ship mentioned in Section 4.1, for instance, comprises a copper tool with a two-sign Cypro-Minoan inscription and thirteen tin ingots, five with two-sign inscriptions, the rest with single-sign texts bearing Cypro-Minoan script signs. Texts with Cypro-Minoan script signs are present also on the lead ingots from a newly investigated wreck near modern-day Caesarea (Yahalom-Mack et al., 2022), though in this case all are single-sign texts. Neither lead nor tin is indigenous to Cyprus. Traders with knowledge of the Cypro-Minoan script would almost

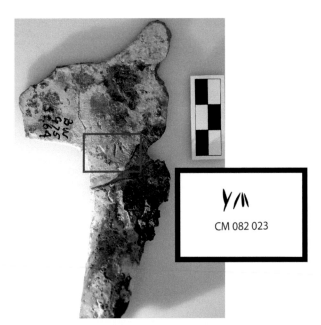

CM 082 023

Figure 19 Incised multisign text on a socketed pruning hook from the Cape Gelidonya shipwreck, B99.

Photograph by John Littlefield, courtesy of the Institute of Nautical Archaeology.

certainly have been intermediaries, ferrying the ingots from their original destinations to Cyprus or elsewhere. As already discussed, the sources of tin in the Late Bronze Age are still debated. Anatolia, Afghanistan, and Cornwall are all plausible sources. The lead of the ingots carried in the Caesarea wreck has been chemically traced to Sardinia. In these cases, the application of Cypro-Minoan texts would almost certainly have been made by middlemen involved in the movement of metals from the edges of the Mediterranean into its interior.

4.2.4 Taprammi and His Bowl

Mobility, interconnectivity, and knowledge of script is evidenced among elites from many different parts of the eastern Mediterranean, not only at Ugarit and Cyprus. The individual relationships developed between traders could have positioned them to survive the collapse of palatial centers with wealth and relationships intact. One reason why Cyprus may have survived the collapse is because of the strong mercantile networks created by its traders that gave them access to goods and traders independent of or at least not whole reliant upon royal networks. An example of a person embedded in such networks is Yabninu. Another similar figure can be found in the person of Taprammi, a Hittite official who traveled widely throughout the eastern Mediterranean and wrote in at least two different scripts (see Figure 20).

Taprammi's voyages, tracked through inscriptions he wrote and literary references to him, provide a means through which to imagine the movements of Cypro-Minoan writers (Hawkins, 1993). An official in the Hittite court, Taprammi wore several official titles, including "Scribe," "Pithos Man," and "Eunuch" (no one does official titles like the Hittites). Like Yabninu, he seems to have also conducted personal business in addition to carrying out his royal duties. According to a tablet from Ugarit recorded in the syllabic cuneiform script, he was negotiating with the king of Karkemish in northern Syria over a personal business deal involving enslaved persons. Taprammi also left a proverbial paper trail in Anatolia. A stone monument inscribed in the Luwian hieroglyphic script in the capital Hattuša is a dedication from Taprammi dated to the reign of the Hittite king Tudhaliya IV (c. 1245–1215 BCE), and Taprammi's seal is on a cuneiform document from the same site.

Another of Taprammi's texts, a bronze bowl also written in Luwian hieroglyphic, reveals him building a network of elites. The inscribed bowl is made of bronze, the appropriate metal for gifts exchanged between persons of equal rank (stone was for gods and silver for kings; Simon, 2018). Befitting bronze, the bowl's inscription is addressed to a scribe of equal rank to himself. The bowl is particularly intriguing for its similarities to inscribed bronze bowls from Cyprus

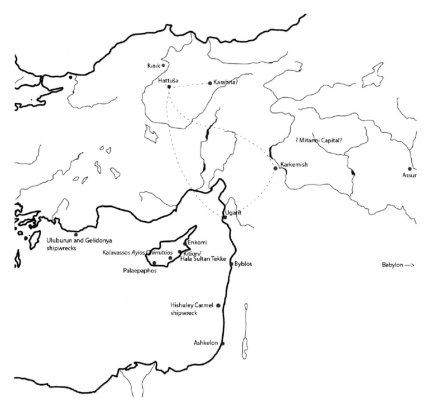

Figure 20 Tracing Taprammi's travels. The map shows places where inscriptions or references to Taprammi have been found. His exact travel routes are not known.

that may even be considered the same document form despite being inscribed in a different script. The formatting of the text on the bowl just below the lip is the same as the inscribed bowls from Cyprus. The biggest difference between the Cypro-Minoan bowls and Taprammi's gift is that his inscription is on a richly embossed bowl carrying complex pictographic imagery, whereas the Cypro-Minoan bowls are simple and undecorated. If they are the same document form, then the function of the Cypro-Minoan bowls can be inferred from Taprammi's: Gifts given between elites, perhaps ones similarly well traveled and interconnected with overseas mercantile activity as Taprammi himself.

4.3 Mercantile Writing during and after the Collapse

How the course of Taprammi's life or that of similar individuals was altered by the collapse of Ugarit and the Aegean palaces is hard to say given the relative absence of deciphered textual evidence dating to the postcollapse period. The discovery of

Cypro-Minoan texts from two sites outside of Cyprus dating to this period, Tiryns in mainland Greece and Ashkelon in modern-day Israel, shows that traders with links to Cyprus maintained and even constructed new trade networks. In the Aegean, Cypro-Minoan texts have been discovered at the site of Tiryns, which is the only palatial center of the Mycenaean world that was substantially rebuilt after the palaces were destroyed. Writers of Cypro-Minoan engaged in overseas exchange show their imprint at Tiryns in the form of mercantile texts on vessels. Copper workshops established in the same areas where vessel texts have been discovered indicate that trade activity at the site was accompanied by the establishment of Cypriots at the site. Fine imported objects from the Levant suggest the community there was entwined in surviving commercial overseas networks.

At Ashkelon, the other place where Cypro-Minoan texts were found post-collapse, the role of traders and writing in the community is less than clear. The label "Cypro-Minoan" for many of the texts there may not even be appropriate. Only a single multisign Cypro-Minoan inscription was found at the site, a two-sign text incised after firing on a nonlocal vessel that petrographic analysis has shown to be from coastal Lebanon or the Akko plain (Master, 2021, cat. no. 51). The vessel's provenance means that the inscription, which was incised onto the vessel handle after firing, could just as well have been made in Ashkelon as elsewhere. In addition to the inscription, there are forty-eight other single-sign vessel texts from the site, including some on Cypriot jars. Ashkelon's vessel-marking practices show some influence from Cyprus, in the Cypro-Minoan inscription and the marked Cypriot vessels, but some of the marks are particular to Ashkelon, and several marked vessels were locally produced, meaning that they were almost certainly marked in Ashkelon. The extent to which Ashkelon vessel markers were indebted to writers of Cypro-Minoan is less than clear.

Three texts on other objects from Ashkelon also speak ambivalently of a connection to Cypro-Minoan writers. The three objects are a wall bracket bearing a single sign, an ostracon painted with an inscription in an unknown script, and a stamp seal bearing an incised inscription likewise written in an unknown script. Wall brackets are found throughout the coastal Levant but have strong associations with Cyprus. Only one other wall bracket text is known from Cyprus (Smith, 2016). The ostracon and the stamp seal are not common Cypro-Minoan document forms, and both bear script signs broadly similar but not identical in shape to Cypro-Minoan signs (McCarter, 2021). It is possible the similarity in the shapes of the sign on the two objects mean their script or scripts could have been derived from Cypro-Minoan, but the inscriptions cannot be classified as Cypro-Minoan.

In contrast to the Cypro-Minoan inscriptions found at Tiryns, which show continuity with writing practices from Cyprus, the Ashkelon texts could speak to disruption. Texts on vessels originating from Cyprus, as opposed to ones produced in the Levant or locally at Ashkelon, all date to the 13th century. Excluding the vessel inscription, which dates to the 11th century, the later texts all have an ambiguous or no relationship to Cypro-Minoan.

It is not clear whether script transfer from Cypro-Minoan ever occurred at Ashkelon. If it did, it could have occurred in the context of trade or by the arrival at Ashkelon of writers of Cypro-Minoan, or individuals with peripheral knowledge of the script may have migrated to Ashkelon. The latter possibility is caught up in debates over the so-called sea peoples and the identity of the earliest "Philistines" whose homeland, according to later biblical accounts, was in the region of Ashkelon and modern-day Gaza (Yasur-Landau, 2010). According to one version of events, a major contributor to the social instability that caused the collapse was a band of marauding pirates or "sea people" comprised of Sardinians, Aegeanites, and Cypriots, among others, who overthrew or at least interrupted Ugarit and the Hittite empire. After destroying the great powers, the marauders settled along the southern Levantine coast, bringing with them an idiosyncratic material culture that combined Aegean, Cypriot, and Levantine elements. The hypothesis that a "multiethnic" group of people, including Cypriots, migrated to the Levant is hotly debated, with scholars of the Levant often more inclined to favor the hypothesis and scholars of the Aegean more inclined to disfavor it.

Whatever the exact course through which Cypro-Minoan arrived at Ashkelon, the differences between writing found at Ashkelon and at Tiryns during the period are indicative of the recalibrations in mercantile relationships in the wake of the destruction of the palatial centers in the east and west. At Tiryns, writers of Cypro-Minoan produced the same document forms as they would have if they were on Cyprus, indicating institutional continuity between the Cypro-Minoan of Cyprus and of Tiryns (Donnelly, 2022b). There are only three certain and two probable Cypro-Minoan inscriptions from Tiryns, but the three definite inscriptions conform to Cypro-Minoan document forms (one clay ball, ##244 TIRY 001, and two vessel inscriptions, ##245 and 246 TIRY Avas 001–2), and they are accompanied by over fifty Cypro-Minoan single-sign vessel texts, indicative of the wholesale importation of the institutions responsible for the production of Cypro-Minoan texts.

The differences in the Cypro-Minoan from Tiryns and Ashkelon tell two different stories about the script's uses during and after, the collapse. At Tiryns, writers of Cypro-Minoan maintained strong ties with institutions on Cyprus, producing typical Cypro-Minoan document forms at a site where Linear B had prevailed until the destruction of its palace. At Ashkelon, writers had only loose, or no, knowledge of Cypro-Minoan document forms, perhaps indicating knowledge loss from the pre- to postcollapse period. Whatever the case, writers of

Cypro-Minoan continued to engage in mercantile activity, carrying their script with them, even as the Mediterranean economy underwent a colossal shift.

5 Landlubbers

A significant portion of Cypro-Minoan texts are not on mercantile objects but on types of objects that circulated almost exclusively within the island, hence the moniker "insular," derived from the Latin for island. Unlike in the neighboring literate societies, where most domestic texts are administrative tablets, most insular Cypro-Minoan document forms are on small, mobile objects and likely record personal names. Small clay balls, the most numerous insular document form, may have been used for sortition, since many are found in temples and are similar to balls used as lots in the Mediterranean from later periods (Ferrara and Valério, 2017). Other document forms are on objects that likely carried social prestige, such as cylinder seals and metal bowls, which we know were shared as gifts between officials in the Ancient Near East (Ferrara 2012). The self-referential, even self-aggrandizing, aspect of insular document forms recalls the mercantile use of writing inasmuch as writing was used to communicate something more than simple administrative information, distinguishing it from the predominant administrative uses of writing elsewhere in the eastern Mediterranean. This self-referential aspect of script use is particularly suggestive given the background of economic upheaval and the transitions of the collapse period in which individual relationships would have had to fill the vacuum left by institutional collapse.

Whether writers of mercantile and insular document forms were one and the same people whose writing habits changed from one setting to another or if they were two distinct groups differentiated by their institutional affiliations is an open question. Some scholars have proposed that merchants comprised a separate social group from the island's nonmerchant political elite, and that the changing political landscape of the collapse period put the two groups into conflict, with merchants eventually emerging as the dominant social force (Knapp and Meyer, 2023). The evidence from writing neither supports nor contradicts this theory. Mercantile texts and insular document forms differ from one another in their formal material attributes, but they share the same basic script framework: They use the same repertoires of script sign shapes, and punctuation. They might be written by the same groups of people who made different types of document forms in different settings or by different groups who learned to write the same script but in different social spheres.

5.1 Who Is Writing on Cyprus (and Sometimes Abroad)

I use the term "insular" to refer to document forms and writing practices bound to the island of Cyprus, as opposed to overseas trade contexts. Several Cypro-Minoan document forms circulated mainly or entirely within the island of Cyprus, sometimes restricted to a single site. Many are document forms attested primarily on Cyprus and not outside of the island. Most insular document forms contain short texts indicative of informal writing contexts. The short texts display diverse paleography even within a given document form, suggesting that the visual expression of writing was not only not regulated but that creative writing displays were encouraged. Although the document forms show some evidence of standardization in their formatting, there is sufficient diversity in other features to conclude that they not in or for administrative purposes or in the context of scribal schools – with two exceptions.

5.1.1 Exceptional Case 1: The Clay Cylinder Document Form

Two document forms fall in neither the mercantile nor insular camp: clay cylinders and the Enkomi tablets (Masson's CM 2). What distinguishes these two document forms from the rest is their relatively high degree of standardized material features. In the case of the Enkomi tablets discussed in Section 3, their near-uniform paleography suggests that they were possibly produced in scribal schools. The clay cylinders, for their part, are widely agreed to be administrative document forms.

There are six examples of clay cylinders from two different sites, five examples from Kalavaso-*Ayios Dhimitrios* (K-AD) and one from Enkomi. The five Kalavaso documents are all contemporary roughly to one another, dating to the LCIIC, found together in Building X, where administrative activity is believed to have taken place. The Enkomi clay cylinder was found in an unclear context and is possibly contemporary to the K-AD cylinders. The clay cylinders are widely regarded as administrative because some contain numerals and lists and were palimpsests (i.e., erased and reused), and because of the administrative setting of K-AD Building X (Smith, 2002).

The clay cylinder writing medium consists of nonperforated, nonhollow clay cylinders approximately 2–5 cm in length and 1.5–4 cm in diameter. Writing on the cylinders runs left to right lengthwise across the long surface of the cylinder, though beyond this similarity there is some variation in formatting among the texts. At least one cylinder, ##101 K-AD Arou 004, contains numerals, and another, Enkomi cylinder ##097, has "many features" suggesting it may "represent a list" (Ferrara 2012, p. 121). In combination with the administrative findspot of the K-AD cylinders, the presence of numerals and lists on the documents supports an administrative interpretation of the document form. Joanna Smith's observation that two of the cylinders are palimpsests, erased and reused for the same purpose, also supports their administrative interpretation (Smith, 2002). Narrowing the focus to K-AD, the clay cylinder document form may be the product of a network of writers who learned how to write in administrative contexts at K-AD. The paleography of the cylinders is distinctive vis à vis both other inscriptions found at the site and inscriptions from elsewhere. The internal paleographic uniformity of the K-AD cylinders suggests that their writers received training in how to construct and write the clay cylinder document form while "on the job" there.

5.1.2 Exceptional Case 2: The Enkomi Clay Tablet Document Form

Limited evidence for the presence of scribal schools on Cyprus comes in the form of three tablets from Enkomi dating most likely to the early 12th century, which Émilia Masson believed were written in a separate subscript CM 2. The uniformity in paleography of the tablets is unique among Cypro-Minoan document forms and includes not just uniformity in sign shapes but also in the ductus and height of the signs. Sign height on all three tablets is around 0.3 cm, with the signs adhering to a strict imaginary rule line. The ductus on all three tablets comprises impressed and impressed-and-drawn signs rendered with a round-tipped stylus, which often created a distinctively Cypro-Minoan "tear drop" ductus.

Martina Polig's 3D models have shown that the paleography of the Enkomi tablets shares features with the inscriptions on other document forms (Polig and Donnelly, 2022, p. 49). A similar combination of drawn and impressed elements, for instance, is used in the construction of sign many forms. What is unique to the tablets, however, is that they have the same paleography across all three tablets. In the rest of the insular documents, and certainly in the mercantile ones, sign shapes within a given document form are varied. The uniformity in sign shape and ductus on the Enkomi tablets would seem to indicate that their writers were following the same rules of representation. It suggests they received the same instruction on how to draw sign shapes, what implement to use to draw them, and how to construct and abide by imaginary rule lines. The obedience displayed by the tablet writers is likely the result of the meticulous instruction and sustained practice occasioned by a scribal school curriculum.

5.1.3 Perishable Materials?

The possibility of a scribal school on Cyprus raises the question of why so few document forms seem to have been produced in scribal schools. The six clay cylinders and three Enkomi clay tablets are the exception and not the rule. Their uniform features suggest, in the first case, training in administrative uses of writing and, in the second case, training in a scribal curriculum. If there were administrative and/or scribal uses of writing on Cyprus, in addition to the mercantile and insular uses, why are there so few examples of them?

One possibility is that clay was not the main writing medium used on Cyprus but that most script was written on perishable materials. Roughly contemporary examples of perishable writing materials include inked wooden writing boards in Egypt, animal skins for Aramaic (Radner, 2011) and wax-coated wooden writing boards for cuneiform (Cammarosano et al., 2019). Wax-coated wooden boards survive in the eastern Mediterranean in only two examples from the Uluburun shipwreck (à la Figure 21). Use of wax-coated writing boards has been proposed as the possible material of choice for Cyprus, since heavy use of wax could also explain another notable absence from the Cypriot record, that of clay sealings (Smith, 2002). Cylinder seals made from precious and

Figure 21 Panels of an ivory writing board dating to the 8th century BCE from Nimrud, Mesopotamia. Wooden boards were more common than ivory.
Courtesy of Metropolitan Museum, 54.117.12a, b.

semiprecious stones, not to be confused with the clay cylinders discussed in Section 5.1.1, were used throughout the Aegean and the Ancient Near East in administrative contexts, impressed into lumps of clay, "sealings," to indicate a seal holder's ownership, authorization, and/or oversight.

If wax was used on Cyprus as a writing medium and sealing surface, then the near-total absence of administrative and scribal Cypro-Minoan document forms could be illusory. It still would not explain, however, why Cyprus used wax for writing and sealing when its neighbors to the east and west preferred clay, or why Cyprus had so many distinctive insular and mercantile document forms. Nor is there reason to believe, given the distinctiveness of Cyprus's surviving writing media, that writers of Cypro-Minoan would have restricted their uses of wax to the anticipated administrative and scribal document forms. Everything we have learned about writers of Cypro-Minoan so far suggests that, if they wrote on wax, they would have written on it in a myriad of ways, displaying the same creativity evident in most Cypro-Minoan document forms.

5.2 Insular Documents Forms

Insular documents forms are characterized by their mix of standard and non-standardized features, their short texts, and in being strongly anchored to Cyprus. The most common insular document forms nevertheless show their writers to be in conversation with writers outside of Cyprus. On occasion, insular document forms are found outside of Cyprus and/or are mimicked by writers of other scripts. Many bear short texts believed to record names of either humans or divinities, or, less plausibly, toponyms. Their mix of standardized and nonstandardized material features indicates that their writers had varied training in how to write and were writing in social contexts in which playfulness with writing was permitted and even encouraged.

There are too many insular document forms to discuss each individually. The most representative insular document forms are discussed in Table 4. The variety of document forms would suggest that writers of Cypro-Minoan could and did decide what to write on, and that those decisions were often local ones. Take, for instance, two gold rings from Kalavasos-*Ayios Dhimitrios* (##165–166) or the three obeloi from Palaepaphos (##170–172), objects not used for writing elsewhere. Each is a document form that is site-specific, unique not just within Cyprus but with respect to the neighboring script traditions as well.

5.2.1 Cylinder Seals (Not to Be Confused with Clay Cylinders . . .)

Cylinder seals made from precious stones are one of the few Cypro-Minoan document forms also used as a writing medium in other regional scripts,

Table 4 List of insular document forms
Only includes writing media with more than one example

Writing media	Sites	Number
Architectural blocks (stone)		
	Kition	1
	Palaepaphos-*Skales*	2
Bronze ring stands		
	Myrtou-*Pighades*	2
Clay balls		
	Enkomi	87
	Hala Sultan Tekke	2
	Kition	2
	Tiryns	1
Cylinder seals (precious stone)		
	Ayia Pareskevi	2
	Hala Sultan Tekke	1
	Kourion	1
	Lattakia, Syria	1
	Palaepaphos-*Skales*	1
	Pyla-Verghi	1
	Salamina	1
	Unknown (Cyprus)	7
Gypsum lids		
	Kalavasos-*Ayios Dhimitrios*	2
Jewelry		
	Enkomi	1
	Kalavasos-*Ayios Dhimitrios*	2
Metal bowls		
	Enkomi	2
	Palaepaphos-*Skales*	2
	Ugarit	1
	Unknown (Cyprus)	4
Ivory rods		
	Kition	2
Obeloi		
	Palaepaphos-*Skales*	3
Oxhide ingots (miniature)		
	Enkomi	3
	Unknown (Cyprus)	1 (Donnelly 2022b, fig. 4.3)
	Total:	**135**

including syllabic cuneiform, Luwian hieroglyphs, and Linear B, but as is often the case with Cypro-Minoan, the document form is reimagined in the hands of Cypro-Minoan writers. The Cypro-Minoan texts are all extremely brief, never more than one word and often only two signs long, and their formatting is wildly inconsistent (see Figure 22). In comparison, syllabic cuneiform texts on cylinder seals found throughout the Near East often record full phrases, usually expressing ownership or obeisance to a deity. The texts are usually original to the seal's composition, placed in panels beside or around the seal's main images. Luwian hieroglyphic seals used by Hittite officials, which include not only cylinder seals but also seals on convex discs, have inscriptions that spread and coil over the entire surface of the seal face. While the content of the syllabic cuneiform and Luwian hieroglyphic texts is not explicitly administrative, the

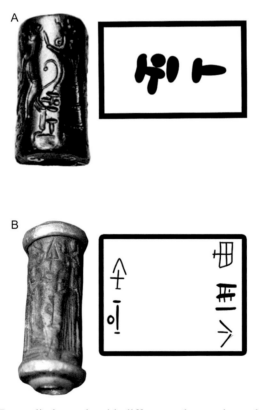

Figure 22 Two cylinder seals with different paleography and formatting. A. ##195 CYPR? Psce 001, h. 2.0 cm; B. ##199 ENKO Psce 001, h. 3.05 cm, two-part inscription. Both parts of the inscription have unusual, unidentified signs that may be decorative and not script signs.

Photographs and drawings by author. Autopsy courtesy of the British Museum.

function of cylinder seals in these contexts decidedly is. Likewise, the Linear B texts on cylinder seals, clay seals, and sealings all pertain to the administration of palatial resources, the types of texts that are remarkably absent from Cypriot contexts. In the Aegean, script rarely appears on seals cylinder but is prevalent on sealings, lumps of clay which, when still wet, were impressed with a seal, incised with an administrative text, and then attached to the object being distributed or otherwise administered.

The exact content of Cypro-Minoan texts on cylinder seals is necessarily unknown, but it is highly unlikely that the texts were meant to convey administrative information. Although some scholars attribute an administrative function to cylinder seals on Cyprus, on analogy with neighboring cylinder seal traditions, the Cypro-Minoan document form is not analogous to neighboring ones, and therefore text content is also likely to be different (Donald, 2016). The texts on Cypro-Minoan seals are often incredibly hard to read, whether on the surface of the seal or rolled out and impressed onto a surface. It is therefore reasonable to surmise that the mere presence of writing was the message, not its content. In other words, the writing was both decorative and semiotic in the same way that seal motifs were (Aruz, 2013). The writing, like the seal images, would convey meaning to the seal's wearer and to viewers of the seal which was separable from and possibly even superseded the meaning of the phonetic word or abbreviations recorded on the seal.

In favor of the decorative interpretation is the utter lack of order or pattern discernible in the placement, orientation, and paleography of the texts. The chaotic formatting indicates a disregard for the potential reader's ability to anticipate where the text on a sealing would be and often resulted in texts that are illegible except under close inspection. The placement of texts on cylinder seals is almost as varied as their imagery. Some texts are arranged horizontally, some vertically, and still other texts are discontinuous, squeezed in between the elements of the image. Some texts are upright on the surface, others upside down; some are legible on the surface of the seal, others only on the sealing surface once the seal was rolled out. Still others might never have been clearly legible given the scatter of signs across the seal's surface. Paleography and ductus are likewise variable. Some texts have a linear ductus. In other cases, the seal carver seems to mimic the shape of signs impressed into wet clay, carving out thick and voluptuous rounded signs (see Figure 22).

Given the willy-nilly features of Cypro-Minoan cylinder seal texts, it might be right to interpret the texts as saying, "here I am, look at me!" and not "name, rank, and title," more embellishment, less administrative ID. The discovery of many inscribed cylinder seals in tomb contexts also lends support to this interpretation of the texts as adornment rather than information. The texts were certainly not the administrative aids they were on neighboring cylinder seals.

5.2.2 Clay Balls

Small clay balls, about 2 cm in diameter, are perhaps the most distinctive and well-known Cypro-Minoan document form, capturing the imagination of scholars and enthusiasts alike with their simple shape and small size (see Figure 23). In a certain sense, the small size and spherical shape of the balls makes them unsuitable to carry texts. Their small size makes them the type of object that a person could easily lose, and the circle shape makes the texts hard to read in a single glance. Often, a ball must be turned between the fingers for the whole text to become visible (Steele, 2014). Yet despite the apparent unsuitability of the clay balls as a writing medium, they are one of the most common Cypro-Minoan document forms, and they seem to have been especially important at the site of Enkomi.

Of the ninety-two recorded clay balls, eighty-seven come from the site of Enkomi, two from Kition, two from Hala Sultan Tekke, and one from Tiryns, Greece. The concentration of balls at Enkomi testifies to their insular character, the peculiarity of their use to Cyprus. At the same time, the lone clay ball from Tiryns raises the possibility that even the most insular of Cypro-Minoan document forms still traveled. In addition, there are two clay balls from Ugarit written in the Ugaritic script, a clear example of a Cypro-Minoan document form adapted to write another script.

Exactly what the balls were used for has attracted much speculation. Suggestions range from weights to gaming marbles to workers' ID cards to lots, inferred variously from the shape and size of the balls, their find-spots, the nature of their texts, or a combination of all three (for an overview

Figure 23 Collection of clay balls of different sizes. A. ##088 ENKO Abou 020 (d. 1.9 cm); B. ##024 ENKO Abou 029 (damaged); C. ##021 ENKO Abou 018 (d. 1.8–2 cm); D. ##023 ENKO Abou 020 (d. 1.3 cm); E. ##022 ENKO Abou 019 (d. 2.3 cm).

Photograph and drawings by author. Autopsy courtesy of the British Museum.

of theories, Steele, 2014). It is generally assumed that all balls had the same function, that is, they are the same document form, because of their consistent material features. The size of the balls is loosely standardized between 1.7 and 2.3 cm in diameter, the texts are always disposed on the ball's central axis, and the ball findspots often are associated with metallurgical production, ritual activity, or both. The standardization of the writing material and formatting is contrasted by their stunning paleographic variation, which includes not only a wide variety of sign shapes and drawing and impression techniques but also writing implements (Smith, 2003). Ball writers were given much leeway when putting stylus to clay as long as wrote along the central axis.

Among the various suggestions concerning the function of the balls, lots used in sortition as, suggested by Silvia Ferrara and Miguel Valério (2017) best, accommodates the evidence. Sortition, a method of resolving questions or making decisions through the casting of lots, was practiced throughout the contemporary Ancient Near East. It is amply attested in the Ancient Near Eastern literary record, but not the archaeological one. In nearby Hittite Anatolia, sortition was used to assign individuals priestly roles for specific festivals or for calendar years (Taggar-Cohen, 2002). Much later, in the Classical and Hellenistic periods, the use of lots to select jurors, assign plots of land, and resolve political disputes is well attested in the literary and, to a lesser extent, archaeological record.

If the lot interpretation of the balls is correct, then the balls inhabit a space somewhere between administrative and nonadministrative documents, an ambiguity reflected in their material features. The balls are standardized in size, shape, and formatting, but the paleography of the texts is not standardized. Similar to administrative tools, the balls might have been used to assign individuals to priestly roles or plots of land but in a manner which by its very nature invites chance. Like much of Cypro-Minoan, the balls and their function elude straightforward characterization.

5.2.3 Reading the Balls Abroad

There is a tentative consensus that the ball texts contain names, derived in large part from comparison to the two balls from Ugarit that record two local Ugaritian West Semitic names in written the Ugarit script (Ferrara, 2012, pp. 111–112). Here, decipherment and analysis of document form converge. Because the Ugaritic balls are undoubtedly modeled on the Cypro-Minoan document form and because the Ugaritic script is deciphered, it is possible to infer the content of the undeciphered Cypro-Minoan ball

texts from them: They most likely record names. Our ability to read,
Ugaritic paired with the concept of document form allows, us to "read"
the content of the Cypro-Minoan balls even as the sounds recorded by the
signs in the ball inscriptions remain unknown. The balls, like the insular
document forms, are at once characteristic of Cyprus but also show the
reach of Cypro-Minoan writers outside of the island.

5.2.4 Metal Bowls

The inscribed bowl document form briefly mentioned in Section 4, like the
balls, consists of texts inscribed onto relatively small, mobile objects, but they
are much less common than the balls (see Figure 24). There are nine Cypro-
Minoan inscriptions on metal bowls, seven made from bronze or copper and two
from silver (the exact composition of the metals awaits confirmation by testing).
Like the balls, the bowls are a largely insular document form that nevertheless
hints at their writers' mobility. All bowls but one, a silver bowl found in a ritual
deposit in the acropolis of Ugarit, were found on Cyprus. The bowl from Ugarit,
a Cypro-Minoan document form found abroad, has a counterpart on Cyprus in

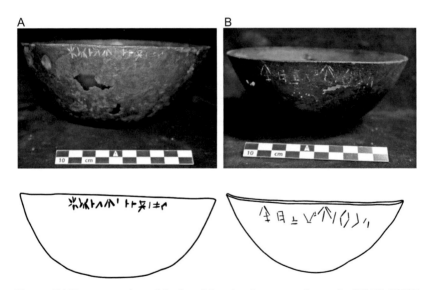

Figure 24 Two examples of the bowl insular document form. A. ##179 CYPR
Mvas 002.

Photograph and drawing by author.

B. ##180 CYPR Mvas 003.

Photograph and drawing by author, courtesy of the Cyprus Museum and the Department
of Antiquities, Cyprus.

a silver bowl found at Hala Sultan Tekke (Yon, 2004). The Hala Sultan Tekke bowl was inscribed in an alphabetic cuneiform script similar to Ugaritic, sometimes called the "short" or "reduced" cuneiform alphabet, fashioned like the Cypro-Minoan document form. It should be regarded as another example of a Cypro-Minoan document form adopted by writers of another script, even if the layout of the text is slightly lower down than on the Cypro-Minoan inscriptions, a difference perhaps attributable to decoration on the bowl's lip (see Figure 24).

The precise social function of Cypriot is difficult to determine from archaeological evidence alone since most bowls were not recovered during archaeological excavation but looted and sold on the art market. A pattern is discernible in the small number of inscribed bowls whose findspots are recorded: Bronze bowls come from tombs, and silver bowls from settlements. Written records from the Ancient Near East record bowls made from various metals being given in diplomatic exchange. As mentioned in Section 4, it may have been the case that different metals designated different levels of exchange: Silver bowls were given to kings, and bronze bowls were exchanged as gifts between officials. It is not clear whether the Near Eastern model applies to the Cypriot one, but the differentiation of the findspots of bowls made from different metals could support a distinction in their function. Comparative evidence from the Ancient Near East further suggests that bowls associated with the elite ritualized consumption of liquids, an activity equally associated with settlement and funerary contexts (Feldman, 2014, pp. 111–137).

The bowl texts, like the balls, show standardization in their formatting but not in their paleography. The standard placement of the texts is, evocatively, just below the bowl's lip. Imagining the bowls were drunk from like a cup, as iconographic evidence suggests, the bowl holder's lips may have touched or covered the inscription as they drank. Alternately, the bowl holder could have drunk from the opposite side, positioning the text in clear view of their companions or the audience of a ritual performance. Unlike the fixed position of the texts, the paleography and structure of the texts vary from bowl to bowl. Some texts have highly linearized signs, others, like the silver bowl from Enkomi and the alphabetic cuneiform bowl from Hala Sultan Tekke, have signs drawn in the "tear drop" ductus characteristic of Cypro-Minoan. The size and legibility of the signs also differs, as does the apparent methods used to make the inscriptions. Variety is also apparent in the structure of the texts: two texts record one sign sequence, five record multiple sign sequences separated by word dividers, and two record multiple sequences, including sign sequences and numerals, separated by word dividers.

The texts are believed to record names, which could support their interpretation as gifts exchanged between individuals. The belief the texts record names derives from several threads of evidence. First, at least four bowls record short sign sequences that end with the sign CM 023, which, as discussed in Section 3, is generally interpreted as a genitive or dative suffix. Second, later Cypro-Syllabic inscriptions on metal bowls, a document form possibly inherited from Cypro-Minoan, record names. If the texts are the same document form, then it is possible to "read" the Bronze Age inscriptions in light of the Iron Age ones. Third, contemporary metal bowls inscribed in other scripts record names of individuals, some of whom, like Taprammi whom we met in Section 4, bear the official title of scribe. Writers of Cypro-Minoan could have been similar highly mobile individuals.

5.3 Cypro-Minoan in the Iron Age

5.3.1 Continuity and the Metal Bowl Document Form

Unlike those who wrote scripts that perished along with their administrative centers, writers of Cypro-Minoan continued to write far past the collapse period and into the Early Iron Age. Bowls are the only Cypro-Minoan document form apparently adopted wholesale in script transfer from Cypro-Minoan into Cypro-Syllabic. The longevity of the document form and its continued relevance even as the political organization of Cyprus underwent dramatic changes in the transition from the Bronze into the Iron Age speaks either to the survival of the institutional settings in which bowl texts were produced and shared or to the artificial replication of an old practice. The evidence is ambiguous.

A bronze bowl from Palaepaphos is the among the latest dated Cypro-Minoan inscriptions, found in a tomb dating from the mid 11th to 10th centuries (Egetmeyer, 2016). The date of the tomb is not necessarily the date of the bowl or the inscription, nor is there any definite way of determining the bowl or inscription date. Its excavators note that the bowl might have been an heirloom, passed down from generation to generation until it was deposited, in which case the bowl would be older than its context. Heirloom or not, the bowl exhibits strong ties with the Bronze Age. Its text, comprising a 5-sign sequence, a numeral, and a 1 + 1 sequence, records the same 5-sign sequence inscribed onto two bowls with secure Late Bronze Age dates (##179 and ##183). It is also similar to another Bronze Age bowl inscription in recording a numeral (##182).

The bowl exemplifies debates over when Cypro-Minoan ends and Cypro-Syllabic begins. At least part of the ambiguity comes from the small number of both Cypro-Minoan and Cypro-Syllabic inscriptions from the 11th–9th centuries. There is no question that by the 8th century, the Cypro-Syllabic script consists of some fifty-five signs, likely a much smaller number than was used in Cypro-Minoan, and that signs shared between the two scripts change shapes in Cypro-Syllabic. It is also clear that Cypro-Syllabic, by this point, is being used to record the Greek language. Many of the inscriptions dating to the 11th–8th centuries, including the Palaepaphos bowl, record signs whose shapes are intermediary, not exact matches for Cypro-Minoan or later Cypro-Syllabic forms (see, for instance, the debate around the *opheltas* obelos, as summarized in Duhoux, 2012). The bowl inscription would be considered such an ambiguous text except for the affinities of its other features to the Bronze Age document form.

When the Palaepaphos bowl was written and by whom raises intriguing questions about continuity in writing practice between the Late Bronze and Early Iron Ages. Were the writers of bowl document forms participating in the same institutional settings from one period to the next? If so, it may have been the same one that mobile, mercantile elites like Taprammi navigated just before the collapse, but reconfigured, severed from its ties to imperial administration and reliant only on relationships between individuals. One piece of evidence in support of this suggestion is the earliest alphabetic inscription found in the Aegean, an inscribed bronze bowl from Knossos, Crete.

5.4 Cypro-Minoan Document Forms and the Alphabet

5.4.1 The Knossos Tekke Bowl

The bronze Tekke bowl from Knossos on Crete, the center of Minoan and Mycenaean Greek administration on Crete until its destruction in the 14th century, is the oldest evidence for alphabetic writing found in the Aegean (see Figure 25). It was found in a tomb dating to the 9th century, but as with the Palaepaphos bowl some scholars have suggested it was an heirloom of an earlier date. The Phoenician alphabetic inscription, positioned just underneath the bowl's lip, records a short text, "the bowl of X, son of X . . ., " which has been interpreted to be either a declaration of ownership or a dedication (Hoffman, 1997, pp. 120–124). Its material features broadly fit the Cypro-Minoan document form, with a slight difference in the placement of the text, which is further below the lip than in the Cypro-Minoan examples. The difference in layout is possibly attributable to the fact that the lip contains other decoration, similar to the Hala Sultan Tekke bowl. Even if the layout were identical to the Cypro-Minoan examples, it would be hard to claim that the Knossos bowl was directly inspired by them. Other Phoenician inscribed bowls date to the 10th century, and the bowl is a relatively popular document form in the Iron Age Mediterranean (Feldman, 2014), often found in tombs like their Cypro-Minoan counterparts. It may well be the case that the Cypro-Minoan document form is the genesis for the inscribed bowls that become

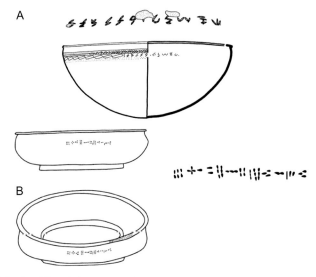

Figure 25 Metal bowl document forms written in different scripts. A. Knossos Tekke bowl with Phoenician inscription. B. Hala Sultan Tekke bowl with short cuneiform alphabetic inscription.

Drawing by author based on Matthäus, 1985.

popular in the Iron Age, but further studies would be necessary to show this is definitely the case.

The Knossos Tekke bowl (named after the location of the tomb) is one piece of evidence for renewed overseas trade conducted between the Aegean, Cyprus, and Phoenicia after a postcollapse lull (Bourogiannis, 2018). According to some scholars, the bowl is of a Cypriot type and must have been produced in Cyprus. Others say that its features could just as well indicate production in the Levant. In either scenario, the bowl is the product of renewed trade between individuals going between the "Phoenician" Levant, Cyprus, and Crete in its use of a document form long-standing on Cyprus and with a possibly contemporary correlate in the Palaepaphos bowl.

The Tekke bowl embodies long-standing associations between the metal bowl document form and mobile individuals involved in overseas trade and "could suggest multi-way influences in the practice of writing between speakers of local languages and speakers of Greek and Phoenician" (Steele, 2019, p. 88). It could well be that the Phoenician alphabet spread in the same type of institutional contexts as Cypro-Minoan itself: networks of overseas traders in which Cyprus played the role of linchpin. On analogy with Cypro-Minoan, the Phoenician alphabet must have been taught and transmitted outside of scribal and centrally administered contexts. Just like with Cypro-Minoan, the script may have also been transmitted in scribal and administrative contexts, but the institutional contexts that facilitated and encouraged the spread of the alphabet throughout the Mediterranean were mercantile.

5.5 Conclusions

The role that Cyprus and its writers played in the spread of writing in the eastern Mediterranean during and after the collapse period has been overlooked. Writers of Cypro-Minoan were involved in overseas networks of highly mobile, literate individuals. Some of these individuals, like Taprammi and Yabninu, were enmeshed in royal and administrative economies but not necessarily reliant on them. Writers of Cypro-Minoan had no such reliance. Even as the sociopolitical organization of the island shifted in response to the collapse, the networks that literate merchants had established allowed them and their script to thrive. In their resiliency and participation in overseas trade networks, writers of Cypro-Minoan can be seen as the template for the spread of the alphabetic script and writing more generally in the early Iron Age.

The case of Cypro-Minoan writers shows how writing and script are a technology that humans can adopt, change, and repurpose outside the confines of scribal schools or administrative centers. Writers on Cyprus invented new document forms and put writing to use in ways that their contemporaries had not conceived of. Their document forms and, more significantly, the mechanisms through which they spread their script, anticipated the spread of writing in the Iron Age, to which all readers of this Element are indebted.

References

Aruz, J. (2013). Seals and the Imagery of Interaction. In J. Aruz, S. B. Graff, and Y. Rakic, eds., *Cultures in Contact: From Mesopotamia to the Mediterranean in the Second Millenium BC*. New York: The Metropolitan Museum of Art, pp. 216–225.

Baroni, A. (2011). Alphabetic vs. Non-Alphabetic Writing: Linguistic Fit and Natural Tendencies. *Rivista Di Linguistica* 23(2), 127–159.

Berger, D., Soles, J. S., Giumlia-Mair, A. R., Brüggman G., Galili E., Lockhoff N., Pernicka E. (2019). Isotope Systematics and Chemical Composition of Tin Ingots from Mochlose (Crete) and Other Late Bronze Age Sites in the Eastern Mediterranean Sea: An Ultimate Key to Tin Provenance? *PLoS ONE* 14(6): https://doi.org/10/371/journal.pone.0218326.

Blackwell, N., Donnelly, C. M., and Hirschfeld, N. (forthcoming). The Inscribed Tools from the Cape Gelidonya Shipwreck. In *Festschrift in Honour of Thomas G. Palaima*. Philadelphia: INSTAP Academic Press.

Bounia, A., Nikolaou, P., and Stylianou-Lambert, T. (2021). Contested Perceptions of Archaeological Sites in Cyprus: Communities and Their Claims on Their Past. In E. Solomon, eds., *Contested Antiquity: Archaeological Heritage and Social Conflict in Modern Greece and Cyprus*, Bloomington: Indiana University Press, pp. 108–130.

Bourogiannis, G. (2018). The Phoenician Presence in the Aegean during the Early Iron Age: Trade, Settlement, and Cultural Interaction. *Rivista di Studi Fenici* 46, 43–88.

Boyes, P. J. (2021). *Script and Society: The Social Context and Writing Practices in Late Bronze Age Ugarit*. Oxford: Oxbow Books.

Cammarosano M., Weirauch, Maruhn, F., K., Jendritzki G., and Kohl, P. (2019). They Wrote on Wax: Wax Boards in the Ancient Near East. *Mesopotamia* 54, 121–180.

Cline, E. H. (2021). *1177 BC: The Year Civilization Collapsed*. 2nd ed. Princeton: Princeton University Press.

Corazza, M., Tamburini F., Valério M., and Ferrara, S. (2022). Unsupervised Deep Learning Support Reclassification of Bronze Age Cypriot Writing System. *PLoS ONE* 17(7), 1–22.

Daniel, J. F. (1941). Prolegomena to the Cypro-Minoan Script. *American Journal of Archaeology* 45(2), 249–282.

Dikaios, P. (1953). An Inscribed Tablet from Enkomi, Cyprus. *Antiquity* 27, 103–105.

Dikaios, P. (1956). The Context of the Enkomi Tablets. *Kadmos* 2(1), 39–52.

Donald, A. T. (2016). Cylinder Seals in Context: An Analysis of Late Cypriot Glyptic. Dissertation. La Trobe University.

Donnelly, C. M. (2022a). Cypro-Minoan and Its Potmarks and Vessel Inscriptions as Challenges to Aegean Scripts Corpora. In P. M. Steele and P. J. Boyes, eds., *Writing around the Ancient Mediterranean: Practices and Adaptations*. Oxford: Oxbow Books, pp. 49–73.

Donnelly, C. M. (2022b). Cypro-Minoan Abroad, Cypriots Abroad? *Athens University Review of Archaeology* 9, 195–206.

Donnelly, C. M. (forthcoming). Cycladic Linear A and Connections between Scripts. In E. Salgarella and V. Petrakis, eds., *The Wor(l)ds of Linear A: Integrated Approaches to Documents and Inscriptions of a Cretan Bronze Age Script*. Athens: National and Kapodostrian University of Athens.

Duhoux, Y. (2012). The Most Ancient Text Written in Greek: The Opheltas' Spit. *Kadmos* 51, 71–91.

Duranti, L. (1989). Diplomatics: New Uses for an Old Science, Part I. *Archivaria* 28, 7–27.

Egetmeyer, M. (2010). The Recent Debate on the Eteocypriot People and Language. *Pasiphae* 3, 69–90.

Egetmeyer, M. (2016). Appendix V: A Bronze Bowl from Palaepaphos-*Skales* with a New Cypro-Minoan Inscription from the Cypro-Geometric Period. In V. Karageorghis and E. Raptou, eds., *Palaepaphos-Skales: Tombs of the Late Cypriote IIIB and Cypro-Geometric Periods (Excavations of 2008 and 2011)*. Nicosia: The Cyprus Institute, pp. 131–136.

Evans, A. J. (1909). *Scripta Minoa: The Written Documents of Minoan Crete 1. The Hieroglyphic and Primitive Linear Classes*. Vol. 1. Oxford: Clarendon Press.

Feldman, M. H. (2014). *Communities of Style: Portable Luxury Arts, Identity, and Collective Memory in the Iron Age Levant*. Chicago: University of Chicago Press.

Ferrara, S. (2012). *Cypro-Minoan Inscriptions. Volume 1: Analysis*. Oxford: Oxford University Press.

Ferrara, S. (2013). *Cypro-Minoan Inscriptions. Volume 2: The Corpus*. Oxford: Oxford University Press.

Ferrara, S. and Bell, C. (2016). Tracing Copper in the Cypro-Minoan Script. *Antiquity* 90(352), 109–121.

Ferrara, S. and Tamburini, F. (2022). Advanced Techniques for the Decipherment of Ancient Scripts. *Lingue e Linguaggio* 2(July–December), 239–259.

Ferrara, S. and Valério, M. (2017). Contexts and Repetitions of Cypro-Minoan Inscriptions: Function and Subject Matter of Clay Balls. *Bulletin of the American Schools of Oriental Research* 378, 71–94.

Fox, M. (2013). *The Riddle of the Labyrinth: The Quest to Crack an Ancient Code*. New York: Ecco.

Galili, E., Gale, N., and Rosen, B. (2013). A Late Bronze Age Shipwreck with a Metal Cargo from Hishuley Carmel, Israel. *International Journal of Nautical Archaeology* 42, 2–23.

Giumlia-Mair A., Kassianidou, V., and Papasavvas, G. (2011). Miniature Ingots from Cyprus. In P. P. Betancourt and S. Ferrence, eds., *Metallurgy: Understanding How, Learning Why. Studies in Honor of James D. Muhly*. Philadelphia: INSTAP Academic Press, pp. 11–19.

Given, M. (1998). Inventing the Eteocypriots: Imperialist Archaeology and the Manipulation of Ethnic Identity. *Journal of Mediterranean Archaeology* 11(1), 3–29.

Godart, L. and Olivier, J.-P. (1976). *Recueil des inscriptions en Linéaire A*. Volumes 1–5. Paris: P. Guenther.

Godart, L. and Olivier, J.-P. (1996). *Corpus Hieroglyphicarum Inscriptionum Cretae*. Paris: Onassaglou.

Goren, Y., Finkelstein, I., and Na'aman, N. (2004). *Inscribed in Clay: Provenance Study of the Amarna Tablets and Other Ancient Near Eastern Texts*. Tel Aviv: Emery and Claire Yass Publications in Archaeology.

Hawkins, J. D. (1993). A Bowl Epigraph of the Official Taprammi. In M. J. Mellink, ed., *Aspects of Art and Iconography: Anatolia and Its Neighbors. Studies in Honor of Nimet Özguç = Nimet Özgüç'e Armağan*. Ankara: Türk Tarih Kurumu Basimevi, pp. 715–717.

Hawkins, J. D., ed. (2024). *Corpus of Hieroglyphic Luwian Inscriptions. Volume III: Inscriptions of the Hittite Empire and New Inscriptions of the Iron Age*. Berlin: De Gruyter.

Hirschfeld, N. (1999). Potmarks of the Late Bronze Age Eastern Mediterranean. Dissertation. University of Texas at Austin.

Hirschfeld, N. (2002). Marks on Pots: Patterns of Use in the Archaeological Record at Enkomi. In J. S. Smith, ed., *Script and Seal Use on Cyprus in the Bronze and Iron Ages*. Boston: Archaeological Institute of America, pp. 49–109.

Hirschfeld, N. (2004). Eastward via Cyprus? The Marked Mycenaean Pottery of Enkomi, Ugarit and Tell Abu Hawam. In J. Balensi, J.-Y. Monchambert, S. Müller Celka, eds., *La Céramique mycénienne de l'Égée au Levant: Hommage à Vronwy Hankey*. Lyon: Maison de l'Orient et de la Mediterranée-Jean Pouilloux, pp. 97–104.

Hirschfeld, N. (2008). How and Why Potmarks Matter. *Near Eastern Archaeology* 71, 120–129.

Hirschfeld, N. (2019). Cape Gelidonya Shipwreck Excavation. In C. Smith, ed., *Encyclopedia of Global Archaeology*. New York: Springer. https://doi.org/ 10.1007/978-3-319-51726-1.

Hoffman, G. L. (1997). *Imports and Immigrants: Near Eastern Contacts with Iron Age Crete*. Ann Arbor: University of Michigan Press.

Humphrey, T. (2022). Power and Diplomacy in the Amarna Letters: Cypro-Egyptian Relations in the Mid-Fourteenth Century BCE. In U. Furlan, T. A. Husøy, and H. Bohun, eds., *Narratives of Power in the Ancient World*. Newcastle upon Tyne: Cambridge Scholars Publishing, pp. 23–46.

Janko, R. (2020). Eteocypriot in the Bronze Age? The Cypro-Minoan Cylinder from Enkomi as an Accounting Document. *Kadmos* 59(1–2), 43–61.

Jones, S. (1997). *The Archaeology of Ethnicity: Constructing Identities in the Past and Present*. London: Routledge.

Karageorghis, V., and Masson, É. (1971). Un bronze votif inscrit (modèle de foie ou de rein?) Trouvé á Kition en 1970. *Studi Ciprioti e Rapporti di Scavo* 1, 237–246.

Knapp, A. B. (2008). *Prehistoric and Protohistoric Cyprus: Identity, Insularity, and Connectivity*. Oxford: Oxford University Press.

Knapp, B. A. and Meyer, N. (2023). Merchants and Mercantile Society on Late Bronze Age Cyprus. *American Journal of Archaeology* 127(3), 309–38.

Markides, M. 1916. Annual Report of the Curator of Antiquities 1914. *Annual Report of the Department of Antiquities, Cyprus*, 5–6.

Masson, É. (1971). *Étude de vingt-six boules d'argile inscrites trouvées à Enkomi et Hala Sultan Tekke (Chypre)*. Gothenburg: Paul Åströms Förlag.

Masson, É. (1974). *Cyprominoica: Répertoires; documents de Ras Shamra: essais d'interprétation*. Gothenburg: Åströms Förlag.

Master, D. M. (2021). Cypro-Minoan Handles. In L. E. Stager, D. M. Master, and A. J. Aja, eds., *Ashkelon 7: The Iron Age I*. University Park, PA: Eisenbrauns, pp. 679–697.

Matthäus, H. (1985). *Metallgefäße und Gefäßuntersätze der Bronzezeit, der geometrischen und archaischen Periode auf Cypern: mit einem Anhang der bronzezeitlichen Schwertfunde auf Cypern*. Munich: C.H. Beck Verlagsbuchhandlung.

McCarter, K. P. (2021). A Twelfth-Century Seal with Three Signs. In L. E. Stager, D. M. Master, and A. J. Aja, eds., *Ashkelon 7: The Iron Age I*. University Park, PA: Eisenbrauns, pp. 669–678.

McGeough, K. (2015). "What Is Not in My House You Must Give Me": Agents of Exchange according to the Textual Evidence from Ugarit. In B. Eder and

R. Pruzsinszky, eds., *Policies of Exchange: Political Systems and Modes of Interaction in the Aegean and the Near East in the 2nd Millennium: B.C.E.* Vienna: Institute for Oriental and European Archaeology of the Austrian Academy of Sciences, pp. 85–96.

Meneghetti, F. (2022). *Miniature Oxhide Ingots from Late Bronze Age Cyprus: An Update on the Material.* Frankfurt: Frankfurter Archäologie.

Monroe, C. M. (2009). *Scales of Fate: Trade, Tradition, and Transformation in the Eastern Mediterranean ca. 1350–1175 BCE.* Münster: Ugarit-Verlag.

Moran, W. L. (2000). *The Amarna Letters.* 2nd ed. Baltimore: Johns Hopkins University Press.

Muti, G. (2024). Discoid Loomweights on Cyprus: New Insights on the Adoption of Practice-related Knowledge from the Aegean. *Levant 56*(1), 50–65. https://doi.org/10.1080/00758914.2023.2297530.

Nahm, W. (1981). Studien zur Kypro-Minoischen Schrift. *Kadmos 20*, 52–63.

Nikoloudis, S. (2010). Multiculturalism in the Mycenaen World. In B. J. Collins, M. R. Bachvarova, I. Rutherford, eds., *Anatolian Interfaces: Hittites, Greeks and Their Neighbours.* Oxford: Oxbow Books, pp. 45–56.

Olivier, J.-P. (2007). *Édition holistique des textes chypro-minoens.* Rome: Fabrizio Serra Editore.

Papasavvas, G. (2023). *Trench Warfare at Enkomi: Personalities, Politics and Science in Cypriot Archaeology.* Nicosia: Astrom Editions.

Parkinson, R. (1999). *Cracking Codes: The Rosetta Stone and Decipherment.* London: British Museum Press.

Peltenburg, E., and Iacovou, M. (2012). Crete and Cyprus: Contrasting Political Configurations. *British School at Athens Studies 20*, 345–363.

Persson, A. W. (1937). More Cypro-Minoan Inscriptions. In E. Gjerstad and A. Westholm, eds., *The Swedish Cyprus Expedition: Finds and Results of the Excavations in Cyprus, 1927–1931*, Vol. 3. Stockholm: Victor Pettersons Bokindustriaktiebolag, pp. 601–618.

Pilides, D. (2018). Menelaos Markides, the First Curator of the Cyprus Museum. In J. M. Webb, ed., *Lapithos Vrysi Tou Barba, Cyprus: Early and Middle Late Bronze Age Tombs Excavated by Menelaos Markides.* Nicosia: Astrom Editions, pp. 8–16.

Polig, M. (2022). 3D Approaches to Cypro-Minoan Writing: Advanced 3D Methods of Documentation, Visualization and Analysis. Dissertation. The Cyprus Institute and Ghent University.

Polig, M., and Donnelly, C. M. (2022). Between Frustration and Progression: An Integrated Cypro-Minoan Signary and Its Paleographic Diversity. *Studi Micenei ed Egeo-Antoloci Nuova Serie 8*, 41–62.

Pulak, C. M., and Matheny R. (2021). The Canaanite Pottery Assemblage from the Late Bronze Age Uluburun Shipwreck. *TINA Maritime Archaeology Periodical* 15, 16–61.

Radner, K. (2011). Schreiberkonventionen im Assyrischen Reich Sprachen und Schriftsysteme. In J. Renger, ed., *Assur- Gott, Stadt Und Land. 5. Internationales Colloquium der Deutschen Orient-Gesellschaft 18.–21. Februar 2004 in Berlin*. Wiesbaden: Harrassowitz Verlag, pp. 385–403.

Rollston, C. A. (2010). *Writing and Literacy in the World of Ancient Israel: Epigraphic Evidence from the Iron Age*. Atlanta: Society of Biblical Literature.

Routledge, B., and McGeough, K. M. (2009). Just What Collapsed? A Network Perspective on "Palatial" and "Private" Trade in Ugarit. In C. Bachhuber and R. G. Roberts, eds., *Forces of Transformation: The End of the Bronze Age in the Mediterranean*. Oxford: Oxbow Books, pp. 22–29.

Said, E. W. (1978). *Orientalism*. London: Routledge & Kegan Paul.

Salomon, C. (2021). Comparative Perspectives on the Study of Script Transfer, and the Origin of the Runic Script. In Y. Haralambous, ed., *Grapholinguistics in the 21st Century-2020: Part I*. Paris: Fluxus Editions, pp. 143–201.

Scancarelli, J. (1996). Cherokee Writing. In P. T. Daniels and W. Bright, eds., *The World's Writing Systems*. Oxford: Oxford University Press, pp. 587–592.

Sherratt, S. (2003). Visible Writing: Questions of Script and Identity in Early Iron Age Greece and Cyprus. *Oxford Journal of Archaeology* 22(3), 225–42.

Sherratt, S. (2013). Late Cypriot Writing in Context. In P. M. Steele, ed., *Syllabic Writing on Cyprus and Its Context*, Cambridge: Cambridge University Press, pp. 77–106.

Simon, Z. (2018). The Recipient of the Bronze Bowl from Kınık. *Ash-Sharq* 2(1), 121–124.

Singer, I. (1999). A Political History of Ugarit. In N. G. E. Watson and N. Wyatt, eds., *Handbook of Ugaritic Studies*. Leiden: Brill, pp. 603–733.

Skelton, C., Selvig L., Chen, D., Srivatsan, N., and Berg-Kirkpatrick, T. (2022). Cypro-Minoan: One Language or Three? An Exercise in Phonology-Based Statistical Analysis. *Lingue e Linguaggio* 2(July–December), 295–309.

Smith, J. S. (2002). Problems and Prospects in the Study of Script and Seal Use on Cyprus in the Bronze and Iron Ages. In J. S. Smith, ed., *Script and Seal Use on Cyprus in the Bronze and Iron Ages*. Boston: Archaeological Institute of America, pp. 1–48.

Smith, J. S. (2003). Writing Styles in Clay of the Eastern Mediterranean Late Bronze Age. In N. C. Stampolides and V. Karageorghis, eds., *ΠΛΟΕΣ . . . Sea Routes . . . Interconnections in the Mediterranean, 16th–6th c. BC: Proceedings of the International Symposium Held at Rethymnon, Crete,*

September 29th–October 2nd 2002. Athens: University of Crete and the A. G. Leventis Foundation, pp. 277–291.

Smith, J. S. (2012). Seals, Scripts, and Politics at Late Bronze Age Kourion. *American Journal of Archaeology* 116(1), 39–103.

Smith, J. S. (2016). A Wall Bracket Fragment with Cypro-Minoan Sign from Kalavasos-*Kaparovouno*. *The Vasilikos Valley Project* 10, 335–336.

Smith, J. S., and Hirschfeld N. (1999). The Cypro-Minoan Corpus Project Takes an Archaeological Approach. *Near Eastern Archaeology* 62(2), 129–130.

Steele, P. M. (2014). The Mystery of Ancient Cypriot Clay Balls. *British Academy Review* 24, 60–63.

Steele, P. M. (2017). *Understanding Relations between Scripts: The Aegean Writing Systems*. Oxford: Oxbow Books.

Steele, P. M. (2019). *Writing and Society in Ancient Cyprus*. Cambridge: Cambridge University Press.

Stroebel, W. C. (2017). Fluid Books, Fluid Borders: Modern Greek and Turkish Book Networks in a Shifting Sea. Dissertation, University of Michigan.

Taggar-Cohen, A. (2002). The Casting of Lots among the Hittites in Light of the Ancient Near Eastern Parallels. *Journal of Ancient Near Eastern Studies* 29, 97–103.

Taylor, J. E. (2015). Wedge Order in Cuneiform: A Preliminary Survey. In E. Devecchi, G. G. W. Müller, and J. Mynářová, eds., *Current Research in Cuneiform Palaeography: Proceedings of the Workshop Organised and the 60th Rencontre Assyriologique International Warsaw 2014*. Gladbeck: PeWe-Verlag, pp. 1–30.

Valério, M. (2018). Cypro-Minoan: An Aegean-Derived Syllabary on Cyprus (and Elsewhere). In S. Ferrara and M. Valério, eds., *Paths into Script Formation in the Ancient Mediterranean*, Rome: Edizioni Quasar, pp. 103–128.

Valério, M. (2016). Investigating the Signs and Sounds of Cypro-Minoan. Dissertation, University of Barcelona.

Valério, M., and Davis, B. (2017). Cypro-Minoan in Marking Systems of the Eastern Mediterranean and Central Mediterranean: New Methods of Investigating Old Questions. In A. M. Jasink, J. Weingarten, and S. Ferrara, eds., *Non-Scribal Communication Media in the Bronze Age Aegean and Surrounding Areas: The Semantics of A-Literate and Proto-Literate Media*. Florence: Firenze University Press, pp. 131–152.

Van Soldt, W. H. (1991). *Studies in the Akkadian of Ugarit: Dating and Grammar*. Kevelaer: Butzon & Bercker.

Vidal, J. (2014). Arthur Evans and the Assyriologists. In J.-L. Montero Fenollós, ed., *Redonner vie aux Mésopotamiens: Mélanges offerts à Jean-Claude*

Margueron à l'occasion de son 80e anniversaire. A Coruña: Ferrol, pp. 141–148.

Vlachek, J. (1973). *Written Language: General Problems and Problems of English.* The Hague: Mouton.

Webb, J. M. (2022). Cyprus's Maritime Connectivity before and after and during the Transition to the Late Bronze Age. In G. Bourogiannis, ed. *Beyond Cyprus: Investigating Cypriot Connectivity in the Mediterranean from the Late Bronze Age to the End of the Classical Period*, Athens: Athens University Review of Archaeology, pp. 23–34.

Yahalom-Mack, N., Finn, D. M., Erel, Y., Tirosh, O., Galili, E., and Yasur-Landau, A. (2022). Incised Late Bronze Age Lead Ingots from the Southern Anchorage of Caesarea. *Journal of Archaeological Science: Reports* Reports 41, 1–10.

Yasur-Landau, A. (2010). *The Philistines and Aegean Migration at the End of the Late Bronze Age.* Cambridge: Cambridge University Press.

Yasur-Landau, A. (2017). Non-Scribal Communication in the Southern Levant during the Middle and Late Bronze Ages. In A. M. Jasink, J. Weingarten, and S. Ferrara, eds., *Non-Scribal Communication Media in the Bronze Age Aegean and Surrounding Areas: The Semantics of A-Literate and Proto-Literate Media (Seals, Potmarks, Mason's Marks, Seal-Impressed Pottery, Ideograms and Logograms, and Related Systems).* Florence: Firenze University Press, pp. 207–220.

Yon, M. (2004). Inscription cunéiforme alphabétique (No. 7001). In Y. Calvet, J.-F. Salles, M. Yon, A, Caubet, and S. Fourrier, eds., *Kition dans les textes: Testimonia littéraires et épigraphiques et corpus des inscriptions.* Paris: Editions Recherche sur les civilisations, pp. 365–366.

Acknowledgments

I would like to thank the many institutions and people on Cyprus who made this Element possible, chief among them the Department of Antiquities, Cyprus, the Cyprus American Archaeological Research Institute, and the University of Cyprus. Individual thank yous are also warranted: the entire ComPAS team (ERC-Grant GA 947749) of sharp, kind women, especially its indomitable leader Dr. Artemis Georgiou, Dr. Lindy Crewe for always being available to answer questions, and Dr Giulia Muti for fruitful discussions. Drs. Kiely and Papasavvas read portions of the draft and improved it. As ever, thank you Sumant Raykar for your partnership.

> Ποιὲς εἶναι οἱ Πλάτρες; Ποιὸς τὸ γνωρίζει τοῦτο το νησί;
> Giorgos Seferis, "ΕΛΕΝΗ"

Cambridge Elements

Writing in the Ancient World

Andréas Stauder
École Pratique des Hautes Études-PSL (EPHE)

Andréas Stauder is Professor of Egyptology at the École Pratique des Hautes Études-PSL, in Paris. His research focuses on the origins and early development of writing in Egypt and in comparative perspective, the visual aesthetics and semiotics of Egyptian hieroglyphic writing, the historical linguistics of the Egyptian-Coptic language, the poetics of ancient Egyptian literature, and Egyptian inscriptions in space.

Editorial Board

About the Series

The study of ancient writing, though not an institutionalised field itself, has developed over the past two decades into a dynamic domain of inquiry across specialisms. The series aims to reflect and contribute to this ongoing interdisciplinary dialogue while challenging schematic views on writing in the ancient world. Written by a team of specialists, volumes in the series will be broadly accessible to students and scholars.

Cambridge Elements ☰

Writing in the Ancient World

Printed in the United States
by Baker & Taylor Publisher Services